MW00653243

THE
ALPHA BET

A SIMPLE GUIDE TO SAVE A COMPLEX WORLD

By: Derek Morrison, Founder of Think Tomorrow Today
Mentor: Satoshi Nakamoto

#AlphaInfluencer #TheAlphaBet #Hindsight2020 #2020theory
#GoodLifeGoals #GameB #Esoteric #ThinkTomorrowToday

Copyright © 2020 by Derek Morrison

All rights reserved

Printed in the United States of America

First Edition

For information about permission to reproduce selections,
contact: contact@3talliance.org.

ISBN: 978-1-7345758-0-4

This book is made from 30% post-consumer waste recycled material and printed with chlorine-free ink.
The acid-free interior paper stock is supplied by a Forest Stewardship Council-certified provider.

For those generations before me who lived, loved and worked tirelessly to build the incredible world we enjoy today. And for my kids who, along with their generation, will inherit the world we are building for tomorrow.

ABOUT THE AUTHOR

Derek Morrison is co-founder of *Think Tomorrow Today*, a 501c3 nonprofit dedicated to advancing society with greater social and environmental responsibility measures. For more than a decade, Derek has also owned and operated a business that helps young children develop social skills and physical literacy. He is part owner of, *XEIA*, an artificial intelligence company designed to give 99% of profits to those in extreme poverty. And he is the creator and writer behind 2020 Theory (www.2020theory.org).

TABLE OF CONTENTS

LETTER TO THE READER

I believe you have a larger purpose than working 1/3 of your life away and worrying about money. You deserve a world in which your attention isn't monetized; a world that respects the symbiotic relationship between all of humanity and nature on this little bright green and blue rock we share within a vast universe. I dream of a world where profit alone doesn't inform decision-making. Instead, creating positive outcomes is the true driver of business and government decisions. And I think something is broken when 80% of humans on planet Earth live on less than $5,000 per year.

Can you imagine a world with not one child suffering from disease or food insecurity? It's now possible. An entire planet with opportunity for each person to become her/his best self is possible. A future that incentivizes you to be healthy and enjoy life to the fullest actually can be the reality soon. Technology and globalization are exponentially advancing and can bring us together if we transform our ways, or tear us apart if we choose to do nothing.

I see a world of abundance and opportunity, but one that has been accidentally siloed away instead of skillfully shared. We are an advanced civilization and we can no longer operate according to rules of the past. The Alpha Bet is a proposal to rewrite the rules, starting with the ways in which you and I can affect change to improve our individual livelihood. You'll find lots of activities and thought experiments to try out in this book, so I recommend having a highlighter nearby so that you can come back to a question or an activity that connects with you, should you not have time at the moment you first read it.

In the following pages, you will find a bit of a different writing style than you may be used to, because I want to make our exchange conversational. You'll find lots of bullet points to sum up various ideas, ellipses for dramatic pause... some CAPS to highlight what's important, plus a sprinkling of profanity and EXCLAMATION POINTS!! Consider these each separately and altogether a wake-up call to see the new world. Or, a slap to your face, if this sounds better. In any case, get ready to realize there are simple solutions to some of the problems we have created as a society. Yes, WE.

You are spending some time and money on this book, and I promise to do my best to use it wisely. The least I can do is introduce myself here. But keep in mind, what really matters is your story. Your trials and tribulation, your experiences and unique abilities are the foundation of the legacy you will further strengthen after today. I hope this book is the "holy shit moment" in your story...meaning that you take one of the actions proposed in this book and create the surprise twist in your life that sets you on a path to true happiness, wellness and balance. This can be the beginning of a brand-new chapter, a chance to shift your life toward a greater purpose, greater substance, and ultimately greater capability to demonstrate your values to the next generation.

For more than a decade, I have been the owner of a small business dedicated to teaching physical literacy and social skills to young children. Previously, I spent years barely scraping by, working tirelessly with little reward, and even had a couple businesses that failed and destroyed my life savings. When things started to finally work out for me and my current business began to support itself, I was able to lift my head out of the paperwork and the stress to really see the big picture. That's when I realized the incredible opportunity and responsibility I have to act on what I have learned.

There has been a few moments in my life that turned my world upside down, but three in particular literally changed my behavior and my entire perception of the world: my dad passing away when I was 10, a solo backpack trip around the world when I was 23, and my children being born after I became 36. Each of those caused me to think deeply about life, purpose and our coexistence with all of humanity. Eventually, I co-founded a 501c3 nonprofit called "Think Tomorrow Today" (dba) "3T Alliance," dedicated to crafting a cultural shift in the way we live, and defining work that reduces stress and suffering, and increases happiness and health.

In preparation for this book, I did research in three academic settings: M.I.T., Singularity University, and Arizona State University. I also met with leaders of various future, technology and social responsibility organizations. Here in these pages I'll explain my findings—the full "bet"—and I hope convince you that a window of opportunity exists for just a few years right now for you, or better said, "us," to either keep operating according to "business as usual," or pause and plan to seize this moment before the window closes.

To be honest, I am not a fan of the title "author," because it shares its etymology with words such as "authority" and "authoritarian," not my favorite positions or approaches. So, let's agree that I am here as the "auctor," the Latin precursor which itself derives from "augere," a Latin verb meaning promote or originate.

I am not here to judge others. In fact, I'm here to absolve you of any guilt you feel. You are now exonerated of desiring to improve your way of life within the constructs and the reality we all share. Self-preservation is at the core of our being; it's not a sin. And we are just playing by the rules of the game...but the "game" is getting revised. Now individuals have the tools to do much more than focus on survival. We now know that elevating humanity as a whole improves our personal wellbeing.

The Alpha Bet is a challenge. Are you ready?

BOOK MAP

The many changes in how we will live, work and consume during the next decade—and the power you have to guide these changes—are wide ranging. So we will cover a lot of topics in a short amount of time. Here, you have a general view of each section of the book, so that you can more easily navigate all the information and come back to certain areas when needed. For quick reference, please find a glossary of terms and an overview of the fundamental concepts at the back of the book.

THE END

The situation right now.... This is where you will find the main "Alpha Bet" and wager. We'll broadly review how we got here and what the future may hold. There are some obvious and some not-so-obvious problems of today in our daily lives—all of which are results of outdated methodologies that will change.

WHO ARE THE ALPHAS?

This is your call to action! Spoiler alert.... You are not the Alpha, but you are the HERO of this story. The world is better because of you, and you will rise above any problems facing you now. In this chapter, we'll examine how the traits of the next generation are our ticket to a better world.

TAKING THE ALPHA BET

Refusal of the call.... Everything may be just fine for those who choose to do nothing, but life could be exponentially better for those who do take action! Do the problems of the world sound too big for you to tackle? Is all this globalization and technobabble overwhelming? If we practice identifying the constructs in our lives that can be altered, then we can take back control of our destiny. You may find that the rules we live by may not necessarily be the rules we still need to live by. We can use the 21st century tools at our disposal to fight for the life we choose. Here you'll find a proposed new society resolution called the "Alpha Agreement."

2020 THEORY

This will be your guiding light.... As your mentor on your journey through the book, this section will provide you the foundation of the 2020 Theory, an explanation of what's happening this decade and which main pillars of society can be reexamined. Plus plenty of eye-opening information, challenges and risks. This will get you ready to start implementing a Massive Transformational Purpose (MTP) in your life before profit-driven technologies decide for us. You can also go to www.2020theory.org to follow along and participate.

PERCEPTION FLIPPING

Time to cross the threshold of your reality.... In this chapter, we take a look at the current challenges the world is facing, with emphasis on the many ways we as humans will personally be able to create opportunities in the place of what might otherwise have been crises. It was Plato who said, "Science is nothing but perception," and together we will change one perception after another. Find a quiet spot, get yourself comfortable and be prepared to see what you have missed, and still not miss what you have seen.

LIFE!

Here we'll bring it back to why you most probably bought this book in the first place. And, how can you talk about life, without getting deep? We'll go down that road and take some time to think about your purpose in life. Is it your job? Will your occupation be around in 10 years? No matter what, there is much hope for a bright future. I'll be your ally, because we're in this together, and I will help you if you need it. Just email me at contact@3talliance.org.

BECOMING ALPHA INFLUENCERS

Approaching and practicing transformation.... You'll find some new frameworks to practice a vision of reality that you may have been missing. After you read this, you can't go back. You are now officially an Alpha Influencer whether you like it or not. Not to worry, it's a good thing and you can take it as far as you like.

ALPHA A.I.

Here's the problem.... We can plan to steer the vehicle of humanity in the right direction, but does it matter who's at the wheel if it's driving itself? We are playing with technologies that we do not fully understand. Artificial Intelligence (A.I.) is offering highly effective solutions to problems that we humans don't have the capacity to understand. Humans are not prepared for what is about to happen, but we should be all right if we play our cards right.

YEAR 2030

The reward…. Year 2030 could be the beginning of a new and improved era for humanity. 2084 may seem like a lifetime away, but the action we take during the 2020s may define many decades to come. In this chapter, we'll blur the lines of science fiction and science reality; and also consider some of the promises of a world with greater Social Capital incentives.

BUILDING A NEW FUTURE

The journey to massive change…. Humans have vastly better lifestyles now than at any other time in history. But, do you feel we've reached our potential? Most businesses and governments are still using 20th century methodologies. Humans have the resources to massively transform the system toward less stress, fewer inequalities, and much more true freedom on a global scale. It's a daunting task to try and change institutions embedded in the fabric of our lives. In the past, an age of change has been marked by a period of disruption of economic and political dogmas rooted in technology advancements (such as agriculture) and expanding globalization and communication methods (such as ships that cross oceans). We are at a historic crossroads once again.

CHOOSE YOUR OWN ADVENTURE

This is the final battle.... This is the moment you can start taking greater agency in the path of your own life. Fight your inner battle of denial, select a tangible Alpha Bet adventure and take action! All of us have the opportunity to physically affect our lives in positive ways that will prepare us for the potentially difficult years ahead. We have to do something, though. We have to act and experience, instead of reading about it. If you sit back and do nothing, reality could hit you with unwelcome surprises. The great news is the world is better off when you are better off, and all it takes is a few micro-actions to alter our behaviors. People and communities are slowly realizing the power they have to change the world. It's easy just to accept the way things are, but it's time we rewrite the rules.

THE BEGINNING

Time to celebrate! By now, you have the tools for greater clarity and confidence to change the world in your daily walk through life. My hope is your mind is free, and you see reality through a new lens. This chapter is a kind of conclusion designed to wrap up and reinforce the main ideas and beliefs of this book, so that as you finish reading you will get its global sense and purpose.

Two notes, before we begin:

1. Data represented in this book change from year to year, and so I have rounded numbers for simplicity and applied the most recent data as of year 2019. Check out the website for updates and to see a gauge

of our progress as a society toward the goals laid out in this book.

2. This edition is focused on USA data primarily, but much of the information can apply to the majority of communities, businesses, and governments globally.

TRANSFORM PERCEPTION

Let us discover our true inner motivations,
reach out to the future, remove the old lens of perception,
and be prepared to see from a new vantage point.

CHAPTER 1

THE END

THE END OF POVERTY, SUFFERING,
DISEASE, DEBT...

THE END OF FINE PRINT, WASTE,
DECISION FATIGUE, PLANNED OBSOLESCENCE[1]...

THE END OF PROFIT MOTIVES,
HIGH INTEREST RATES,
ADVERTISING, DEADLINES...

THE END OF REACTIVE FIXES, FEAR, CONTROL,
MODERN WARFARE, THE ANTHROPOCENE[2]...

---

1   A legal practice (in U.S.) and policy of certain businesses that produce consumer
    goods that rapidly become obsolete due to frequent changes in design, termination
    of the supply of spare parts, and the use of nondurable materials.

2   A period of time (2.6 million years ago to the present), characterized as the time in
    which the collective activities of homo sapiens began to substantially alter Earth's
    surface, atmosphere, oceans, and systems of nutrient cycling.

THE ALPHA BET IS THIS...

WE HAVE ENTERED A NEW ERA IN WHICH YOU HAVE GREATER POWER THAN EVER TO CHANGE THE ENTIRE WORLD. GO ALL IN, REALIZE YOUR TRUE CAPABILITIES AND TAKE ACTION.

Artificial Intelligence is learning our desires and altering its algorithms for businesses, government, and communities to adapt accordingly. We have the opportunity to code the best future possible by challenging conventional wisdom and truly behaving in a way that aligns with our values...before it's too late. Ultimately, **The Alpha Bet** predicts that the Alpha Gen will play an emergent role in designing the future. They will wield increasingly unparalleled technological powers.

THE WAGER:

If you lose the bet? Nothing new. Everyone for themselves. You continue to work to survive while inequalities and ecological problems become even larger global issues.

If you win the bet? More happiness. More health. A life of true purpose, and a dynamic, transformative mindset in greater harmony with an evolving world.

We often operate according to conventional wisdom, cultural lessons and standardized education that has helped to develop our **perceptions, finances, lifestyles, surroundings, workplaces,** and our **citizenship**. All these aid us in making sense of the world and forming routines that seem to work for everyone. We older humans are comfortable in our routine and resistant to change, but the Alpha Gen can still be molded. Most of us are going about "business as usual" and accidentally perpetuating global social and environmental problems. The Alpha Gen will also propagate the lessons and norms they see around them and will apply those principles to the constructs of tomorrow. We still have time to teach and influence the Alpha Gen to think massively differently—with a global perspective, to protect all of humanity and to build a better world. Knowingly or not, we are all Alpha Influencers in some way or another. And we must begin to augment our perceptions, finances, lifestyles, surroundings, workplaces, and our citizenship.

In a hundred years, no doubt we'll have different problems. The data revolution happening now affords us the opportunity to do a better job at preparing for and mitigating potential problems in the future. The algorithms derived from data today can identify the difference between correlation and causation and can predict potential consequences and 2nd order consequences[3] (as well as 3rd, 4th, and 5th order consequences, for that matter) of any opportunity with unforeseen costs. But we need immediately to deal with the problems of

---

3   (a.k.a. Second-Order Effects) Are outcomes that are different than the first desired outcome yet are directly related to the initial decision. Every decision has a consequence and each consequence has another consequence.

today. We live in a world of astonishing abundance and new capabilities, but we still operate according to old rules. We all know there are many problems in the world today, but you may not be aware of all the solutions in development now. Know this: the end (of primitive reasoning) may be near and the future is actually looking bright!

GOOD NEWS ABOUT THE APOCALYPSE

A new theory (albeit not a popular one) is that dinosaurs died from their own methane gas release. Literally, there could have been so many huge animals burping and farting methane into the stratosphere that they altered the habitable global temperatures. So, good news is we don't have to worry about that. Bad news is it's an ironic metaphor for our huge cars, cows, and coal industries expelling unnatural amounts of dangerous gases.

There have been five mass extinctions of plants and animals on Earth over the course of the last few hundred million years. It's been about 65 million years since the last one. And, we are currently under way with our sixth mass extinction[4], evidenced by massive losses in biodiverse

---

4 An ongoing extinction event of species during the present Holocene epoch as a result of human activity. The included extinctions span numerous families of plants and animals. *Notably, this extinction is happening at a faster rate than all other mass extinction events before on Earth.

habitats globally on land and under the sea just in the last 100 years...not to mention climate science measuring increased levels of greenhouse gases causing atmospheric changes.

ENVIRONMENTALLY, the good news is we know dinosaurs weren't smart enough to fix their gas problems. We know that humans are now on Earth during this epoch, and we are pretty damn smart. We have the capability and the tools to work together and fix problems to ensure our survival. Granted, it is widely believed the sixth mass extinction has been accelerated due to human activity, but for the most part, humans have gone through the early stages of change, starting with denial, and now we're at the point of acceptance and ready for action.

SOCIALLY, many studies have found that violent crime and also mortality from disease or crime are all at the lowest they have ever been (per capita) since the beginning of time.

So, let's talk about the world getting better. Our minds are 10 times more likely to pay attention to bad news than good news. This is the formula that news agencies use to keep the money coming in...to keep your attention in a competitive landscape.

What else?

Decreased extreme poverty rates globally; near exponential growth of the number of charity organization being founded; hundreds of major cities across the globe creating sustainable infrastructure, many under the aegis of the United Nations Sustainable Development Goals

(UN SDGs)[5]; large investments from the wealthiest people in the world to tackle the world's problems; and businesses refocusing from shareholder needs to ESGs (Environmental - Social - Governance) needs including mandating sustainable suppliers and hiring for Corporate Stewardship roles.

There are amazing innovations happening daily. Nanotech and enzymes that can eat ocean plastics, better and cheaper electric car batteries, electrolysis to desalinate ocean water for consumption, solar panels that can store power and also pull potable water out of the air, A.I. that can help build more efficient cities, drones that can plant more carbon-eating, oxygen-breathing trees and healthy foliage along coastal lines...the list goes on.

We're going to be all right. The apocalypse on Earth may hold off until the sun dies out in a few billion years—at which time we will probably have figured out galactic travel. Work is being done to mitigate or solve all other existential threats to our existence that we know about. And—if not— then why bother worrying about it? Don't worry about everything going to hell. Worry about what you can do to give your life more substance and meaning—then DO IT— and if, after a while, you don't like it, no problem. Do something else. Do something different every year of your life if you want. So long as you've been **respectful** of others, **learned** something new, and increased your **network**, then you have just added substance and more meaning to your life and ultimately to the world. So enjoy the journey. If

5   The 17 Sustainable Development Goals (SDGs) developed in 2015 and adopted by all United Nations Member States, are a call for action by all countries to promote prosperity while protecting the environment.

everyone does that, and they do it through the eyes of the Alpha lens—conscious of what is truly good for them—then the world will continue to improve.

THE END OF "BUSINESS AS USUAL"

Government and businesses are most effective when the populace fears an existing problem that needs to be dealt with. Whether it is resource scarcity, lack of jobs, economic crisis, climate change, epidemics...it's an accidental model for success—a construct, not a conspiracy. It can be changed.

Don't feel ashamed if you haven't been living the way you want to. It's just a symptom of modern society. The Alpha Bet aims to diagnose the underlying conditions so that we can all do our part in treating the causes that lead to despair, inequalities, human rights abuses, and ecological destruction.

You are just following the script we've been provided. Study hard, then work hard; play hard; when you can, pay bills. Then someday when you're old and retired, you can live free from work and do what you please. We can now change the script. During this transitional period between 2020 and 2030, governments, businesses and the Alpha Gen will be observing our behaviors. We want them to know that humanity wants to thrive, to be healthy, and motivated to bring progress to all of humanity and its caretaker, the Earth. We are not meant to have our labor be so undervalued, or

7

to lead a life filled with drudgery between the hours of 9:00 AM and 5:00 PM, Monday through Friday.

And so, we do need to voice our opinions and act according to our true values. We should take a monthly (or annual) pause to consider if the things we buy and trash truly make us happy: is an attitude focused on self-preservation bringing me joy, or am I just following "the script" half the time?

With the advent of advanced technologies, governments and businesses are again unknowingly and accidentally using those advances to perpetuate a traditional (and traditionally winning) algorithm that can be illustrated this way:

REACTIVE ACTION + CONTROL + FEAR
= MONETARY PROFITS

The landscape of government and business has changed though, and the old way does not work. Technology has advanced so much that we as individuals have access to an immense pool of information. The more information we get, the more say we have about the outcomes. Profit can no longer be a ubiquitous gauge for success. The new way is:

PROACTIVE ACTION + COLLABORATION + RESPECT
= SOCIETAL PROGRESS

This is the way forward for the majority of humans to continue to survive on Earth. The old way is broken and has reached its end. You and your community can protect each other and demand change using your consumer purchasing power and online feedback, your vote, and your individual and collaborative actions—all expressions of your aspirations.

You have the power to hold businesses and governments accountable. Never before have societies been this informed, this aware. Never before have societies felt this much power.

Change is a given. We will not get better without it. We will not learn without it.

Here are three arguments about the impending societal changes that require forward thinking.

1. **You and your community need to be ready for a transformation in work.**

   Many jobs can easily be replaced by Robotic Process Automations (RPA) or other types of technology (software) soon. What does this mean?

   - Multiple studies indicate nearly half of all job types globally are at risk of being replaced or at least augmented by technology before the year 2030.
   - This could lead to more desperation and more crime.
   - One way to mitigate this in your neighborhood is to spend more time and money strengthening your local philanthropies, learning about Community Foundations and Community

Development Financial Institutions (CDFI), and also supporting alternate forms of income such as crowdsourcing, freelancing and other "Gig Economy" jobs.

2. **Businesses that survive the coming decade need to transform now.**

The coming years will likely be very challenging for most businesses. Business operations will need to shift toward more transparency and greater attention to stakeholder needs. Plus customers are beginning to call out businesses that only quantify profit bottom lines rather than triple bottom lines (TBL)[6] such as measuring the business impact on PEOPLE (improvements in society and employees' wellness), PLANET (environmental protection and regeneration of resources), and PROFIT (economic strength to leverage business capabilities).

• Behemoths like Amazon and other large corporations are merging to create online oligopolies[7], thus rapidly making the current concept of "small business" something from the past.

6   An accounting framework with three parts: social, ecological, and financial. Some organizations have adopted the TBL framework to evaluate their performance in a broader perspective to create greater business sustainability and value.

7   A market in which control over the supply of a commodity is in the hands of a small number of producers.

- There may even be more currencies to consider such as Social Capital[8], cryptocurrencies, personal data, or even foreign currency.
- More than three billion people will gain reliable Internet access for the first time in the coming decade...so, your business could potentially cater to an entirely new market somewhere else in the world.
- Ultimately, the rising businesses of the near future will deal in relationships and network-building rather than focus on profits. This means that creating more and more stuff, using hard selling and manipulative advertising, squeezing human labor for maximum efficiency at lowest cost, and using planetary resources without replenishing the resource will all be faux pas. Consumers will celebrate the businesses that are worthy of their trust. They will also want the power to customize their experience if they choose, and to connect with other people who share their passions and values.

3. **Governments need to adapt to a more connected, globalized society.**

   The script is flipping. People across the world are realizing they have more power than their governments do. Together, the exponential increase in most

---

8 Any activity considered good for society. Often refers to a form of measuring levels of trust, cooperation, sharing, volunteering, and relationship building.

technologies and rising ecological problems have reached an inflection point where progress will move even quicker. Consumers and businesses are taking actions to bypass traditional economic and political frameworks. Governments will have to speed up, become more dynamic, and act accordingly. Changes in employment (and employment conditions) will affect tax revenue and distribution. What will these changes trigger?

- Innovative ways for your local and national governments to make money, such as through a technology tax[9].
- Wider acceptance of alternate currencies such as Ethereum and Bitcoin.
- More and more exclusive online economies and "virtual nations[10]" popping up with various citizenship benefits and rights earned in exchange for a fee or personal data.

If only a few people demonstrate change, and everyone else conducts "business as usual," then we truly may be on a path to planetary devastation.

---

9   A fee that a government imposes on any company that replaces a significant number of human workers with technology, such as machine learning software or robotic process automation (RPA).

10 Online (or Extended Reality) communities that spend money, time, volunteering, data, or social capital cryptotokens in exchange for citizenry. Citizenship can include an array of benefits such as cybersecurity, education, transportation partnerships, guaranteed highest quality products, food and water security, crime and property insurance, no interest loans, and emergency safe havens like micronations or bunkers.

We won't know for sure before it's too late, due to the Overshoot and Collapse[11] process. A Sustainability Strategy professor at M.I.T. (affectionately nicknamed "Dr. Doom" by his students) wouldn't offer an exact prediction, but reluctantly told me some of his colleagues are convinced the year 2050 is the point of no return if things don't *drastically* change during the 2020s.

To express the idea as a standardized amount, **humans need to double their efforts if we are going to create a flourishing planet for generations to come.** Those humans in the most economically developed countries (MEDCs)[12] need to lead this change. It is imperative to reduce carbon output by at least 50% and spend twice as much time on socially responsible activities by year 2030. Anything less could skate our species to the edge of extinction and will almost certainly cause increased stress and decreased "happiness set-points" globally.

Countless businesses are taking a "stakeholder orientation" approach, which is a big step in the right direction to strengthen communities with social responsibility measures rather than perpetuating the old notion that business must be oriented toward increased profit margins. For example, when the issue is carbon and other greenhouse gases, there are lots of governments and businesses not only dedicated to reducing the gas output, but also offsetting it with advanced

---

11 (similar to "Malthusian catastrophe") occurs when a population's demand on an ecosystem exceeds the capacity of that ecosystem to regenerate the resources. One example is the ecological collapse of the original inhabitants on Easter Island.

12 "most economically developed countries," which are sovereign states that have a developed economy and advanced technological infrastructure.

innovations like skyscrapers that filter air as it passes through as well as much simpler solutions like planting trees.

The key for all this to work and get to the level of sustainability we really need as a species is simple participation from society. The more people who share these ideas, purchase only from responsible businesses, and advocate for systems that preserve and strengthen our humanity as their primary purpose, the more innovations will develop to ensure greater planetary harmony for us all to enjoy.

YOU AND I HAVE THE POWER NOW TO SHIFT THE POTENTIAL NEGATIVES INTO A FAVORABLE FUTURE FOR US ALL. WE ARE THE CONSUMERS TO WHICH GOVERNMENT AND BUSINESSES RESPOND. THEY ADAPT TO OUR CHOICES, NOT THE OTHER WAY AROUND.

A shift in mindset is all it takes. Shift your primary purpose and motivation for success from "Accumulation and Profit" to "Altruism and People." This means we need to immediately:

Become Alpha Influencers for social change and ensure our employers have an officer or committee dedicated to imbedding societal and environmental elevation into the DNA of the business. Net Impact (www.netimpact.org) and Conscious Capitalism (www.consciouscapitalism.org) are two organizations that can help you form a committee at work.

Use consumer purchasing power to support companies that spend *at least* 1% of their total revenue on philanthropy. A full 1% of total revenue spent on philanthropy is scarcer than you think in business. Even 1% of net revenue is uncommon in business. One place to find those that do go above and beyond can be found within any of the numerous Corporate Social Responsibility (CSR) indices. An example is the Benefit Corporation Directory.

Prepare to vote for politicians and local authorities who will reduce waste and support the Sharing Economy[13] and Social Capital innovations. This part ensures that, at a governmental level, policies and actions are aimed at improving social standards, living conditions and quality of life for all.

This will be the defining decade in our human history. There are many ways to achieve these objectives including the actions and adventures you'll find in this book, such as taking the "Alpha Bet" and applying the "2020 Theory" in your life.

"Business as usual," conformed routines, manipulative marketing, inefficient politics, and financial/legal complexities have all distorted our present vision. You are one of only a few who know about The Alpha Bet and the 2020 Theory now. This is your formal invitation to become a *mindful* Alpha Influencer with us. Machines and algorithms are substantially influencing the Alphas as well, and so to clarify some, we are "Human Alpha Influencers." Live in the blur or

---

13 An economic model defined as a peer-to-peer (P2P) based activity of acquiring, providing, or sharing access to goods and services that is often facilitated by a community-based online platform.

begin to see with 20/20 clarity. It's up to you now. **Together we can change the outdated rules.**

Some things to consider as you proceed through the book and think about the script, the rules and constructs we live by:

Economic tipping points may be near as indicated by the extreme financial inequality of the 1% vs 99% scenario. How will the creation of more alternate currencies, such as cryptocurrencies, play into this and can you see yourself purchasing crypto-anything?

Societal issues like social media addiction and an increase in General Anxiety Disorders could be affecting you in more ways than you know. Plus with deepfakes[14] on the rise, will society be even more easily manipulated? And how will increasing human displacement due to war and natural disasters affect you?

Environmental tipping points may be near and becoming more and more obvious (irreversible biodiversity loss and nitrogen levels, for example, along with a possible overshoot and collapse day on the horizon). Have you noticed or been impacted by the changing climate yet?

Technological advancements, such as A.I., automation, and robotics, are improving exponentially, making the world more efficient and creating new opportunities; but also taking jobs at a faster clip than we can retrain workers and learn new income opportunities. How will this affect people

---

14   A technique for human image synthesis based on artificial intelligence. It is used to combine and superimpose existing images and videos onto source images or videos with a high potential to deceive.

in your community, and how will your neighborhood and nearby businesses adapt?

Globalization trends bring to anyone with a phone instant awareness of issues anywhere in the world (and also create new job markets and expanded customer opportunities). Consider the fact that between 2020 and 2030 nearly THREE BILLION more people will gain Internet access, creating billions more products and the clutter they bring, but also billions more potential customers for your talents. Are you going to focus your energy on connecting with those in your immediate vicinity or reach out to a global audience regarding subjects such as information, education, and personal income and expenses? (There's really no right or wrong answer; it's a personal preference).

Enterprise/capitalism is changing with more and more oligopolies gobbling up mid-size businesses and small businesses struggling to stay afloat. To succeed, new business models are quickly updating to be more transparent, sustainable, agile, and network-focused. How will this affect your place of work?

- **Profit** may (very arguably) be responsible for the massive inequalities of today, which could mean it will be replaced as the primary success metric. What should the purpose of businesses be, and what metrics can be used to measure progress?
- **Advertising** has exploded in recent times. It is sophisticated and uses psychology to manipulate us into buying lots of stuff that becomes useless shortly after purchase. It's also causing

societal issues like decision fatigue[15], clutter, and decreased mental bandwidth. How can we combat this?

Political extremes that engender greater divides won't be bringing humanity together in a global kumbaya anytime soon. How do we use technology to keep the peace, maintain the natural order of positive and negative forces, and customize governance to the individual to create a more connected and more virtual world?

THE END OF 20TH CENTURY THINKING

There is a wave of change coming, with automation at work, bioengineering of living things, driverless vehicles, drone deliveries, virtual reality social media, being only the most obvious examples. To me, and I'd bet to you, this can sound overwhelming. Yes, you can choose to just go with the flow, and all will probably be fine. The primary message of this book is that you have the opportunity to be more than just "fine." The key is how to identify the changes that will directly and indirectly affect your life. Your actions during the 2020s decade will determine the life you live in

---

15   The deteriorating quality of decisions made by an individual when faced with too many choices.

the 2030s. For example, A.I. is monitoring your behavior online and will be feeding you advertisements that align with your behaviors. Do you want advertisements that direct you toward spending money on products that offer little to zero long-term happiness? Or can you trick online search engine and marketing algorithms into suggesting products, processes and services that will result in lasting changes to your life and the world for the better? (The answer is "yes" you can trick the algorithms).

Imagine a world where you have the time, the health, and the resources to enjoy life to the fullest, to learn anything you want, and to discover your highest potentials. A world where helping others is valued more highly than personal wealth. A world of fewer advertisements and more mental clarity, less paperwork, fewer lawsuits, and more common sense. In fewer than 10 years, you could be working no more than three or four days per week and have all this among healthier and happier people and on a planet that tracks that health and happiness growth.

The Alpha Gen is already learning how to end problems of the 20th century and to perpetuate a new, better lifestyle for humanity as early as year 2030. We just need more people to influence the Alphas to follow through and expo-nentiate our values into the way we operate individually and as a global society.

CHAPTER II

WHO ARE THE ALPHAS?

"THESE BRAND-NEW TECHNOLOGIES, METHODOLOGIES, AND HUMANS ARE THE TICKET TO A BETTER WORLD."

VISION FLIP

Out with the old FIXED MINDSET.
In with the new GROWTH MINDSET.

Alphas are not necessarily dominant, highest ranking, or top dogs. Alphas in this book refer to the FIRST IN A SERIES. We are experiencing a lot of newness and "alphas" in the world today, as humanity embarks upon a new beginning. It is true that change is uncomfortable if not downright scary to lots of folks, but we need to spread the word that these brand-new technologies, methodologies, and humans are the ticket to a better world.

I like to think the Greek letter Alpha represents Abundance. Is the future going to just be an abundance of stuff, advertising and profit? Or, are we at the beginning of a new world—one that will be abundant in individual health, purpose, belonging, and harmony? It's up to you to think with a fresh outlook, which I like to call "Alpha Vision"; or, in other words, remove any boundaries in your thinking and challenge the 20th century mindset.

Learning the **alphabet** was a fundamental start to the way you communicate today. Similarly, all of humanity is learning a fundamentally new way to operate, thanks to alpha technologies. There has been a great awakening of issues economically, culturally, and environmentally on a global scale. Humans are more connected than ever before and are evolving with help and augmentation from Emerging Technologies (EmTech)[1]. This is an incredible time of innovation and collaboration powered by these technologies, until now only dreamt about.

Appropriately, the alpha generation humans are in their own right proprietors of great power, global perspective and socially responsible tendencies inherited from their mostly Millennial parents. People **born between 2010 and 2025** are generation alpha. Their predecessors, generation Z (a.k.a. Zoomers) are entering the workforce now, and we are learning how the dynamic and fast pace technology advancements during their upbringing affected their behaviors and mindset today.

---

1   21st century technologies reshaping life as we know it. Examples include: quantum computing, Artificial Intelligence (AI), Extended Reality (XR), Robotic Process Automation (RPA), drones, 3D printing, smart sensors, smart contracts, autonomous vehicles (AV), alternative fuel, biometric ID, synthetic biology, bioprinting, Voice-user Interface (VUI), Brain-computer Interface (BCI), and MUCH more. *Notably includes new tech industries: PropTech (property), FinTech (financial), EdTech (education), FemTech (female), MadTech (Marketing), InsurTech (insurance), WealthTech, LegalTech, FoodTech, AgeTech...you get the trend.

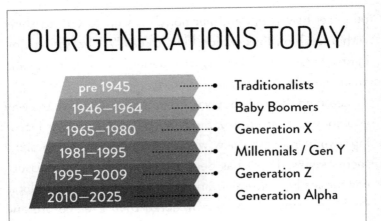

OUR GENERATIONS TODAY

pre 1945	Traditionalists
1946—1964	Baby Boomers
1965—1980	Generation X
1981—1995	Millennials / Gen Y
1995—2009	Generation Z
2010—2025	Generation Alpha

Alpha Gen is just now beginning to join our race and just beginning to learn from us all. Your actions this decade will help determine their future behaviors and beliefs as their intellects develop.

Regardless—this book is about the opportunity for you to influence the direction of massive change in the world by simply thinking differently and changing some of your own habits. This book is not about children. This is your story. You are living in a time of unprecedented transformation—and you can design the future you want.

This book is about **YOU**.

You hold great power. You can and will influence many Alphas by your example. Synchronously, you've got a decade to make your values a reality before the markets shift and provide for the needs, desires, and incomes generated by the Alpha Gen. In 2030, your place of work and your mindset may be left in the dust if you don't adapt to their ways.

I have been on a journey to learn about what is really behind all this simultaneous transformation in business, sustainability, environment, and society. The big answer (from a 10,000 foot view) is exponential technological advancements. This has led me to join some future fore-casting groups such as the World Future Society to help identify the trends that will have the greatest impact in our lives. I believe if you can see change coming, you can better prepare to take control of what it will do to your life. And if you want to show others, then you must demonstrate a new way forward by being the "doer." It is virtually impossible to change someone's mind by just telling. Just do it!

TECHNOLOGY AND THE ALPHA GEN

Since at least 2010, all of us have been using some of these exponential technologies transforming our world. I have gone so far as investing in an Artificial Intelligence company in its infancy. This company, called "XEIA," is the first ever A.I. company registered as a Benefit Corporation. I use XEIA at my primary place of work to improve our administrative processes. Since 2010, I've owned a business dedicated to teaching children age 15 months and older the fundamentals of both physical motor skills and social skills. Having A.I. to manage many of our backend processes allows us to improve the quality of our classes, because we can spend much more time out on the frontlines with the customers.

That experience has taught me that Alpha Gen youth are highly intelligent for their age. They are better at making decisions than many adults. The oldest of the Alpha Gen (birthed in early 2010s) understand world societal and environment problems better than some adults. The whole generation has grown up with more advanced educational and emotional learning tools than any before them.

They are generally good at sharing, have impressive coordination, and at an early stage in development, they are beginning to show a drive for meaning and purpose. Consider this: the great wealth transfer[2] will mean many Alphas will have anything they need without a focus on money. And, their guardians are teaching them the difference between what they "NEED" and what they "WANT."

Even at age 10, these juveniles are influencing others in social media and they are developing some amazing and entertaining content. They don't need to start businesses or even be involved in large corporations; they already are comfortable participating in the sharing economy.

Alpha Gen has been trained from day one to be lifelong learners...and they are hungry to learn more. They are at once surprisingly independent and learning that when they collaborate with others (especially others who are not like them) they get even better results. They seem fearless and are being taught to always be creative in problem-solving.

---

2   The period of time between 2020 and 2040 during which 45 million U.S. Baby Boomers are presumed to transfer more than $60 trillion of wealth (collectively) to their children.

Money is not sacred to Alpha Gen yet. To most of them, expensive toys are no different from the boxes they come in. The Alpha Gen does well with cool new tech, but ultimately, they prefer their guardians get off the phone and play with them.

Agile and comfortable with change within a set of boundaries or structured rules, they seem to speak the truth with little filter; and it's awesome. Yes, they are still young as I write this, but they are being taught to be aware of the world of deepfakes and misinformation in which they —and we— live. They are keen bullshit detectors, and it will be interesting what this means 20 years from now.

They've got it right. The Alpha Vision mindset requires experiential learning and real life practice, but it works. Experience has taught me it can take only a few weeks of consciously identifying the limitations we set on the world around us to begin integrating a new way of thinking that, in turn, introduces a new mode of operation that works within (and gradually alters) the existing systems.

The **Beta Generation**, born around year 2026 to 2040, may be super intelligent, but their knowledge will be based on the world we are starting to create today.

EVOLVING HUMANS

In addition to environmental changes, gene editing (including biohacking[3]) and globalization are affecting physical human evolution. The way we process information is evolving too.

Picture the days when you were young. Take a couple of minutes to scan through your memories as far back as you can all the way through high school. What were the weekends like growing up? What games did you play with friends during the week? Did you do any after-school activities? What was your favorite part of school? What was your least favorite?

Children and teens are playing, learning and maturing in an entirely new world...or worlds, for that matter. With Extended Reality (XR)[4] worlds as well as video game worlds, young minds may soon have trouble separating the physical from the virtual. If you haven't played a Virtual Reality (VR)[5] game in the last couple years, you should try it out! The technology has improved significantly, and it feels very real. Forms of Extended Reality can be used for pure entertainment, or for good, or for bad—as I'm sure you can imagine.

---

3   Biological experimentation (as by gene editing or the use of drugs or implants) done to improve the qualities or capabilities of living organisms especially by individuals working outside a traditional medical research environment.

4   (a.k.a. cross reality) Is an all-encompassing term for technologies that bring digital objects or sensations into the physical world (Real Reality - RR) or vice versa. Examples include Mixed Reality, Virtual Reality, Cinematic Reality and Augmented Reality, Cyborg Intelligence, wearables and sensory interface technologies.

5   A fully immersive computer-generated experience using purely real-world content (360 Video), purely synthetic content (Computer Generated), or a hybrid of both typically viewed through special VR goggles along with wearable technology.

Some time ago a story circulated about a dad who hired an online assassin to kill his son's video game avatar and thereby curb the boy's game addiction. The question arises: Are video games an addiction similar to adults' addictions to their job? Kids can actually earn a lot of money gaming, but it takes time, practice and dedication to make it to the top—just as it is difficult for professional athletes to achieve their status. Esports for example is a billion-dollar global industry where people earn big money for playing video games. If you don't know about this yet, you will soon.

Recent (2019) research has found semantic memory (general knowledge about the world), episodic memory (recalling details of specific experiences), and specific skill specialization seem to be on the rise. On the other hand, crystalized knowledge (arithmetic and vocabulary, for example), certain types of critical thinking (i.e. analytical thinking), and broad skill capabilities seem to be declining.

Maybe our brains are just making room for a new kind of intelligence since we don't have to rely on memorizing many things from the simple (a friend's phone number) to the complex (Planck's Constant). This can be seen as good or bad—but overall it's potentially an evolution of our mental constructs. There is a known phenomenon happening now called the "Google Effect" (a.k.a. digital amnesia). It happens when you forget certain information that can easily be accessed online. Chances are that forgetting stuff isn't an indication of getting dumber, just an indication of thinking differently.

So you can use that concept next time you forget your keys or forget to do a chore…."I didn't forget; my thinking is just evolving."

Consider: will humans ever get to a point where no person knows how things actually work? For example, important mathematical theorems and scientific formulas fundamental to the operation of everything from your microwave to pharmaceuticals to transportation can easily be found and explained online. Say someday humans lose electricity and have no understanding of math and science fundamentals. It would be difficult to ascertain all the knowledge of today from books—assuming those are still around.

Our human curiosity and drive to explore and progress typically lead us to test out anything we can think up. If the good guys don't do it, then the bad guys will gladly figure a way to serve their own self-interest and profit. To ensure that any idea (1) will be positive for all people and the planet and (2) has long-term viability is to give children the mindset and the methodology to make it happen.

THE FUTURE OF EDUCATION

Educators know their system needs an overhaul to properly prepare kids for tomorrow, especially considering the technologies of today. High school, for example, is an important time in brain development, but often a huge missed opportunity. It was for me. I just wanted to fit in like many high school kids do, and made lots of bad decisions. Imagine what the teenagers today go through with their lives on social display, plus the amount of distractions and digital manipulations they face. Obviously there's work to be done to address the current issues of depression, violence, and increased suicide rates in American high schools.

It is now scientifically proven that experiential learning is *the* best way to learn. We also know that kids build stronger cerebral connections when their brains produce "happy chemicals[6]" from a variety of movements such as the ABCs of Physical Literacy (Agility, Balance, Coordination, and Speed). We know that the old ways of forcing kids to get up too early for their age-related circadian rhythm, feeding them an unhealthy lunch, and having them sit in classrooms most of the day listening to lectures is not the most conducive environment for learning. We have always known that all kids are different; we now realize that affects appropriate choices in how we deliver learning that lasts. The 20th century methods are slowly morphing toward a more customized solution for each individual child.

In the near future, the most effective educational methods will no doubt focus on developing different skills. Why memorize something that can easily be found online? Important skills of the 21st century may instead include: active listening and focus, self-actualization and creativity,

---

6   The four neurotransmitters in our brains most often associated with feelings of happiness: Dopamine, Oxytocin, Serotonin and Endorphins (DOSE).

long-term thinking, emotional intelligence, biomimicry[7], learning how to learn, exploration, serving others, compassion, simplicity, systems thinking[8], and collaboration.

Today's world is rich with countless pioneers, both institutions and individuals, forging a new way to think about education. On the organizational front, these three are a good beginning:

- The Collaborative for Academic and Social and Emotional Learning (CASEL)
- The Equity Project, LLC
- Synapse School of California.

Some of my personal favorite people in education right now are:

- Co-founder of Socos Labs Vivienne Ming PhD researches the use of A.I. to develop an endogenous motivation to learn and live happily without the need for incentives and rewards (like money) to succeed. She calls this practice "Incentive Insensitivity[9]." (And the current title she gives herself on LinkedIn is "professional mad scientist.")
- Educational Consultant Kayla Dornfeld MEd works to improve EdTech, redesign classrooms

---

7   The science of applying nature-inspired designs in human engineering and invention to solve human problems.

8   The opposite of "binary thinking." It involves several iterations of an idea and considers the way that a system's components interrelate, over time, and within a larger system. One example is "human centered design thinking."

9   Coined by Dr. Vivienne Ming, it is a form of internal motivation to act regardless of external factors like money or reward. It is a necessary component for successful athletes to "get in the Zone."

for flexible seating, and set up situations in which students are leaders and teachers are students (a.k.a. reverse mentoring).

- Pediatrician Laura Jana MD focuses on developing "Qi skills" during toddler years to prepare children for life skills such as self-control, reading body language, being a lifelong learner, determination, taking action, learning from failure, and imagination.

- Professor of Psychology at Stanford Carol Dweck PhD researches brain plasticity and how we can train ourselves to live with a growth mindset (open to criticism and learning) rather than a fixed mindset (believing your talents are limited).

- Founder of JR Storytellers Jason D'Rocha writes children stories designed to teach human creativity, critical thinking, mindfulness, adaptability, collaboration, awareness, intention, empathy and compassion.

ALPHAS MUST BE GUIDED TO LOVE HUMANITY

What really matters is life and love. I've come to realize that LIFE happens when you're off the computer and spending time with friends and family. Life happens when you're playing, traveling and experiencing new things...

not when you're at a desk working. Not when social media shoots you up with a hit of dopamine every time someone likes your photos. Life happens when you use your talents to help others and elevate humanity. I believe this so much (and wanted to engrain it in my memory) that I tattooed a representation of all this along the right side of my body. Alas, a good life today typically is inadvertently played out as doing what everyone else is doing, working exhaustively and making as much money as you can. The questions the Alpha Bet aims to "solve for" is this:

How do we individually take control of the paradigm?
How can we decouple our concept of happiness from money?
And how can we live a life of greater purpose?

The paradigm of the way we live, work and consume is up for debate and will be changing as we begin this new alpha world. Things are already changing, right? Do you see it? Research suggests the **2020s decade** will be a major pivotal moment in human existence. An "Age of Transformation."

In these pages, I'll offer you a new version of reality you can choose to accept, or not—then it's up to you to live according to the old pre-alpha principles we live in today... or to embrace and help guide the principles we're already learning from Alphas in this new world. Repairing our individual viewpoints, thinking globally, and taking action to change our programmed modes of operation will help accelerate big societal changes. I just ask you stay open to new ideas as we progress through this book, and the new ideas taking hold right now in society around you. Some of the more **controversial big picture topics** I'll touch on is:

- **Individual income caps:** Capping individual income at 100 times the annual median *household* income (a voluntary pledge at first, then eventually normalized)...but grandfathering in those who exceed that amount already.

- **Giving more:** Every person giving at least 100 hours of *time* per year to virtual or in-person volunteering...but making four-day work weeks the new normal (with the goal of achieving two-day work weeks and reconceiving philanthropies after year 2030).

- **Business marketing reduction:** Spending 50% less on advertising...but increasing brand awareness via community support and increased philanthropy.

- **Business profit ceilings:** Starting with a consumer demanded 20% reduction in profits with a goal of capping profits at 5% as a standard ethos across all nations...and distributing the excess among low level employees, low income communities, or philanthropies at the discretion of the business.

- **Government military reduction:** Spending 10% less on military mostly by eliminating outdated 20th century technologies...but spending more on local and global health, education, and housing infrastructures.

- **Guaranteed Basic Needs:** Introducing a new currency called "Social Capital"...but it can only be earned and used with services deemed good for society, such as services that provide for health, education, shelter, clean water, and healthy food. Think of it as "Good Money."

These aren't entirely new ideas. We just haven't been able to accomplish these concepts because societies haven't had the power to mobilize like we do today—combined with the amount of accessible resources and technology in the world at this moment in time. We just need more people to see and experience that "what is good for the WORLD is best for ME."

There will always be a fight between good and evil. For example, **everyday** there are hundreds of content moderators working to block thousands of disturbing images of terrorism, rape, murder, suicide, and child exploitation on sites like Google, Facebook, and YouTube. It's so bad that some of the moderators have developed PTSD. There are now A.I.s like "Clearview" that have the capability to search millions of profiles to automatically search, destroy and possibly convict online platform violators. Regardless, these defenses can only temporarily deter the bad guys. Likely, there will be bad actors who create similar technology to seek and destroy, or vilify, good social media profiles.

The Alpha Gen is no different. The resources and technologies we have now and that of the future can be used for more good than bad; but we must embrace it, be personally protective, and be especially proactive against those who will use it for evil. Our relationship with the Alpha Gen is a symbiotic one. We depend on them to make the right choices in the near future, but they are not a scapegoat for how the world turns out after this pivotal moment has passed. You and I are responsible for engineering the foundational principles the Alpha Gen will perpetuate.

TRANSFORM FINANCES
Time and attention are the most valuable currency.
Use it to find balance in life, and beauty in the world
around you. Let us thoughtfully plan for success to bloom
an enriched life. A life that targets actions that are good
for the world and not just good for us individually.

CHAPTER III

TAKING THE ALPHA BET

"RETHINK THE WAY YOU INTERACT WITH THE CONSTRUCTS OF SOCIETY, CONSIDER IF OUR RELATIONSHIP WITH MONEY IS HEALTHY, AND HELP DRIVE THE MOMENTUM AND CHANGES HAPPENING NOW FOR A BETTER WORLD."

VISION FLIP

Out with the old FIXED MINDSET.
In with the new GROWTH MINDSET.

The way in which we live, work and consume will look different as we enter the next decade. The transformation occurring now is called **Globalization 4.0**[1]. If you choose to take The Alpha Bet, it's a matter of accepting that things are changing and then changing your personal frame of mind during the 2020s decade. Rethink the way you interact with the constructs of society, consider if our relationship with money is healthy, and help drive the momentum for a better world.

1   Term coined at the World Economic Forum Davos 2019 summit describing the complete digitization of the social, the political, and the economic—changing the way that individuals relate to one another and to the world at large.

Taking the Alpha Bet means stepping outside of our comfort zone and challenging the leaders and the systems that operate on "proven" philosophies and methodologies. An Alpha Bet is the acknowledgment that change is necessary, and the RISK is if we continue to operate according to old school rules and old ways of thinking. It is a commitment to change something about ourselves so that we will ultimately make the world better in some way. If we don't take the bet (or subscribe to a similar philosophy), then we risk selfishness becoming the norm and the eventual erosion of humanity.

There's no denying the more we humans collaborate to make the world a better place, the better it becomes. And the better the world becomes, the better your personal story becomes. That is the essence of The Alpha Bet.

After doing research for this book, my belief is we're going to be all right and things will improve, especially after year 2030. But everything could be *way* better if we take control of our lives this decade and guide the communities, businesses and governments in the right direction. The years leading up to 2030 will be full of change, so we need to be agile and be open to adapting to the transformation.

IDENTIFY THE CONSTRUCTS

Constructs such as personal and community **social networks**, **economic systems** on micro and macro levels, and **political frameworks** will all be gradually transforming over the course of the 2020s.

Our ideas of community, business, and government have changed considerably over the last few centuries, and it's time to change again. Your experience with all these is subjective, and you can step into a new reality. The more of us who shift the lens through which we view the world, the more acceptable it will be to integrate fully into the true and improved version of reality.

Our idea of business is just a theory. Some businesses centuries ago transacted in shells, many focused solely on agriculture, and most were part of merchant collectives. Today there are billions more people in the world with billions more products and services from which to choose. And the business framework is to compete for consumer dollars and attention with the end goal of accumulating maximum revenue and profit margin. **One day businesses may be entities that are purely designed to elevate society and Earth,** considering all stakeholders and facets of the supply chain without a need for profit at all.

The concept of "community" once primarily described people geographically near you who help to ensure survival of the land, yourself and your family. Now, various types of communities exist. You may never know or even see your neighbors, but you are active in one or more of the virtual communities online. One day, community could be customized to provide for every individual need with the help of A.I. and robotics.

Same goes for our idea of government. Each nation has been practicing its model of government, and over time different theories have branched out. A long time ago the purpose of government was to provide for and strengthen the monarchy. More resources, more servants, and more territory were considered progress. If you're reading this in English, you probably agree with me that Communism and Dictatorship models are inevitably faulty and should not be considered a viable political ideology. Now various forms of political democracy mixed with economic capitalism rule for the most part, especially in the West. And, it's evident that the cracks in this theory are starting to show. No matter the system, eventually the loopholes will become too great, and it will be time to shift. All nations can and must one day cooperate to guarantee basic needs are met for all humans and will exist to protect the survival of the planet.

The United States federal government is designed to promote the welfare and safety of its citizens. It ensures emergency services, safe roads to travel, safe food to eat, protection against crime against person and property, and military defense. It also sets the legal rules in this game of life you participate in. It has moved beyond the original idea of the Framers of the U.S. Constitution a bit by also providing a military offense and what some leaders consider national economic stability, a development that has been controversial.

If we view governments, businesses and communities through the lens of their present-day constructs, then technically, you don't have to participate in any of them. But life would be difficult and sad for most people without participating and using the resources, rules and structures in place. The constructs are incredibly useful and important to our well-being, but they are now at an inflection point and change is inevitable. Someday soon we'll live in a world with a better version of these constructs. Maybe further into the future the world may have no need for these constructs at all...but one thing is for sure, they are ever evolving and adapting.

REFINING THE SOCIAL CONTRACT

It's about time we add an amendment to the way we operate as a society, primarily because technology and businesses both play a new role in our world. If you see the changes coming and you are willing to take the Alpha Bet, then I submit to you the following "Alpha Agreement."

The Alpha Agreement is the foundation of 2020 Theory. It is a modern refinement of the 17th century theory developed by Thomas Hobbes and commonly called the "Social Contract." He thought of society as a "leviathan" that was in charge of influencing the constructs we all live by. A leviathan that, today, has great power to treat the underlying problems of modern society and heal the world. His theory described what rights all humans should have (no matter what) and how these inalienable rights can be maintained and nurtured in harmony with political authority.

Among the many theories and governmental systems that derive from the Social Contract are the U.S. Declaration of Independence and the democracy to which it gave birth. Another is the United Nations Universal Declaration of Human Rights created in 1948. You can find a full description at http://www.un.org/en/universal-declaration-human-rights. And in 2006, B Lab, an organization formed to serve people striving to use business as a force for good, created a simple yet effective Declaration of Interdependence: www.bcorporation.net/what-are-b-corps/the-b-corp-declaration

The Alpha Agreement is designed to give society the tools and the resolve to lift you up, support your goals, and protect your God-given rights in the 21st century.

THE ALPHA AGREEMENT

We the Inhabitants of Planet Earth, in Order to form a Healthier, Happier, and Safer world, do ordain and establish this Agreement to give permission to and influence the next generation of decision-makers to alter the constructs of the past to protect Humanity for the future.

Guaranteed Basic Needs shall include adequate healthy food, safe shelter, clean air, clean water and effective sanitation for all humans.

Social Capital Systems shall be available to incentivize good citizenship in exchange for modern Ancillary Needs funding such as education, healthcare, utilities, transportation, Internet access and insurance.

Resource Abundance in the environment is imperative by way of Governing the Commons[2], ethical technologies, and supporting the U.N. Sustainability Development Goals (SDGs).

"Smart" Governments must use the wisdom of crowds[3] to lift their people up, distribute resources more equitably, and reduce complexities. A government must be agile, diverse, and use Systems Thinking methods to consider long-term consequences.

Limited Business Excess in Profit, Advertising, and Individual Income extremes by way of calculated economic ceilings.

The Purpose of Business is to transparently provide resources and networks for People to be their best selves while protecting

---

2   When a shared natural resource is governed to allow for collective common good and regeneration rather than self-interest and resource depletion. Coined by Nobel Prize Winner and Economist, Elinor Ostrom.

3   (a.k.a. Crowd Intelligence) Is the idea that large groups of people are collectively smarter than individual experts when it comes to problem-solving, decision making, innovating and predicting.

the Planet and ensuring Natural Capital[4] regeneration.

Workers' Responsibility is to work to the extent that they find joy in what they do; and to add value to the world, their lives, and their places of work (in an effort to achieve the above Purpose of Business).

Consumers' Responsibility is to demand the development of goods and services that respect and benefit society, economy and the environment throughout the life of the good or service.

Media Purpose is to purely seek and provide accurate and transparent FACTS; not for profit, not for sensationalism, and not for ratings.

Reward Altruism and respect humanity defined as assuring ALL humans will be treated fairly, be kept safe, be offered strengthened human connections, and have the opportunity to become their best selves.

Human Progress is to live more than you work, to create more than you consume, to have "freedom of attention[5]," and to pursue a life that is balanced. Progress requires the opportunity to explore our personal capabilities and passions with Experiential Learning so long as we do not infringe on these same rights of others.

Massive Transformation is necessary at least every 100 years, but it can be thought out and phased in to benefit the early adopters, and to avoid disrupting the lifestyles of those not comfortable with change.

---

4 The world's stocks of natural assets which include its geology, soil, air, water and all living things. It is from this natural capital that humans derive a wide range of services, often called ecosystem services, which make human life possible.

5 Coined by Dr. James Williams, co-founder of Time Well Spent campaign, it is the belief that technology should be designed to improve our lives and help its user achieve their goals...NOT to achieve more clicks or engagement with the technology itself.

The Alpha Agreement requires slightly changing the constructs to which we have grown accustomed to. Do we follow the will of a handful of people in power, or do businesses and governments truly operate according to the will of the people? Do you feel more like a leviathan or a lemming?

Change is not easy, and that is why we need to have a clear view of where we are heading and what transformations a revised Social Contract can bring to us and to all. Keep an open mind. We can make the world better *with* or *without* technology. But if we do embrace the inevitable new automation and technological advances, then we can amplify our power and keep up with the rapid pace of change.

SOCIAL PROGRESS MENTALITY

Globalization 4.0 is the light at the end of a decade-long tunnel ahead. With the right structures in place, Globalization 4.0 can alter the mechanism to distribute wealth. Individuals can earn their fair share by way of income from work PLUS Citizen Social Capital Points[6] primarily from philanthropy.

---

6   A doctrine that the capitalist system does not distribute sufficient income to keep
    itself in operation; and must issue national dividends, free basic needs services,
    and/or a monetary equivalent distributed in exchange for participation in activities
    deemed good for society.

Wealth in this system is measured in Social Progress rather than corporate or individual profit. What would the world be like if the word "wealth" were redefined? Someday it could even include a score calculated by A.I. and tracked on a blockchain[7] based on how much good you provide for society minus how much bad. This wealth calculation can also be kept private just like you can keep your finances private today.

The Harvard Business School's Social Progress Index defines **Social Progress** as:

> *The capacity of a society to meet the basic human needs of its citizens and communities to enhance and sustain the quality of their lives, and create the conditions for all individuals to reach their full potential.*

One can argue that if a large corporation has two million shareholders, then is it not elevating society? My counter is that it may be slightly elevating those people who can afford the shares and are advantaged enough to have an investment portfolio. Overall, publicly traded companies are driven to focus primarily on profit, which is generated by developing more stuff and squeezing the budget to have the largest margins possible. Every decision is calculated based on achieving excessive financial gains first; and then possibly achieving happy, healthy employees and communities second (if there is a financial case for that).

---

7   A system in which a record of transactions (such as smart contracts or cryptocurrency) are maintained across several computers that are linked in a peer-to-peer network.

Corporations may have a responsibility to *shareholders*, but many companies are coming around to the fact that their responsibility to *stakeholders* is of greater importance. Just in time too, since everything is becoming more and more automated. Shareholders these days are by and large just "renters" of the shares until stock-bots trade the shares grounded on algorithms the humans never see. Stakeholders, on the other hand, comprise the employees, the customers, the community and anyone or anything else directly impacted by the business operations.

Speaking of automation, conservative estimates show that upwards of 47% of the jobs we know today in the world are at risk of being replaced by machines before year 2030. There will be new industries and jobs created globally, some say more, in fact, than those taken over by technology; but by and large, the predictions are that workers will become independent "gig" workers. For a more seamless transformation, we will need to put in place greater societal support constructs, such as Social Determinants of Health (SDOH)[8]. For you, this means two very important things:

1. You will still be able to earn a living < BUT you must save time for volunteer work.
2. Your cost of living will go down < ONLY if business profits are regulated.

"Regulation" is a scary word for many people. Government regulation in the wrong place can stifle innovation and create

---

8   Identifying and preemptively improving neighborhood environments, economic stability, education, access to medical care, and behaviors toward health on a hyperlocal and individual basis.

undue complexities. The profit margins of automated busi-nesses will continue to fatten, leaving more environmental and societal problems in the wake unless the business has an Ethical Automation policy in place. Many workers will find new jobs that pay some of their bills, but they may need a few years to truly make ends meet again. This will be a critical emergency, and the government will need to step in. Political and economic pendulums will swing away from regulation once ecology and poverty problems are mitigated to reach a more sustainable level.

Total government control is definitely NOT the solu-tion. Carefully and selectively regulating certain extremes is the goal. The good news is many businesses have already started shifting their practices to increase "Triple Bottom Line" metrics without government intervention. Examples include 181 CEOs of the Business Roundtable committing to change the purpose of a corporation from focusing on profit as the primary bottom line metric to the purpose of focusing on communities, customers, employees, suppliers and shareholder benefits as all equally important to profit. Many powerful companies like Goldman Sachs are mandat-ing all businesses that they take public must have a diverse board of directors with a focus on women. And, the world's largest asset manager, BlackRock, is requiring companies they invest in to improve social responsibility and environ-mental sustainability. These are huge milestones in trans-forming the concept of business as we know it.

Equal distribution of wealth will not work. An equitable imbalance is the necessary goal. Instead of 80% : 19% : 1%

wealth distribution, we can work toward a distribution of wealth that more closely resembles a bell curve—20% : 60% : 20%.

Imagine the scales slightly more balanced. Imagine a world in which **20%** (not 80%) of humans live under $40,000 (but have basic needs guaranteed), **60%** make between $40,000 and $100,000 per year (beyond basic needs), and **20%** earn between $100,000 and $6 million (based on year 2020 dollars). The resources exist to make this possible today. The more people who switch to a Social Progress Mentality (or in other words, take the Alpha Bet) the more power we have to demand this shift be allowed to occur.

PROGENITORS OF MODERN TIMES

$6 million. There, I said it. If you reach a $6 million per year salary, are you okay with stopping there and giving everything over and above away each year, or will you need more personally?

Lots of people dance around the idea of an income cap, but no one ever gives an actual number, because they are afraid of being demonized as anti-freedom; or put in an economic, ideological or political box that disagrees with free-market capitalism; or branded as a socialist or unpatriotic, or whatever. The urge to immediately disparage any idea that diverges from the status quo is a "conditioned response." It is a short-sighted gut reaction that has been learned over time from our elders and is pervasive in the media and many institutions. Is it too much to ask to cap INDIVIDUAL annual income at 100 times the nation's median household income ($60,000 times 100 = $6 million)? **Not wealth or assets**...just 100 times the **annual income** per average HOUSEHOLD essentially. Die-hard economists who follow Milton Friedman's theory still get to have their extreme wealth in the world, but not as much extreme poverty. The idea is people who have earned more than $6 million before an income cap rule is instituted will be grandfathered into their way of life—no judgment.

This means anyone climbing up the corporate ladder, for example, will not be able to climb higher than $6 million annual income (ideally including the total of all income, business ventures, benefits, perks, etc). Yes, it is difficult to track or to transition to this without loopholes and fraud. And it's virtually impossible to mandate at this point, but we need a starting point. We need a calculable, tangible vision for the businesses of the future, and conscious consumers willing to join in on an Alpha Bet.

Do we not live in a time of extreme financial inequality locally and especially globally? We've tried everything else—better technology, tax incentives, grants, more rules and more complexities, and most of it has done wonders—but the fact is the inequalities are still way too huge and a cap is an easy solution. Organizations could distribute the excess money previously allocated to big salaries among employees and the community.

Former U.S. Secretary of Labor and current professor of public policy at UC Berkley, Robert Reich, says extreme wealth often stays concentrated in high-end products and services, and sits in investments, while a considerable amount is also spent on lobbying and paying off politicians in order to ultimately dictate the rules of capitalism. As he puts it: "Let's [change] the way the economy is organized. Now this doesn't mean confiscating the wealth and assets of the super-rich, but [instead] creating a system in which economic gains are shared more widely."

It's difficult to exactly calculate what monetary effect on goods and services such redistribution would engender, and maybe that's part of the reason no one has suggested a specific income cap amount. Roughly, the math adds up to 50 trillion dollars that could filter to the populations most in need, over time. If that entire amount were distributed equally among every nonprofit business, then each of those nonprofits would have to deal with 1,000 times as much revenue. Not a bad problem to contend with. Another way to look at it is by dividing 50 trillion among the six billion poorest humans on Earth would instantaneously double their incomes. What would you do with a 100% raise to your annual income? Transferring money directly to those in need is an especially tall order, however, and the money might not continue to circulate within those communities. Allowing the money to filter through businesses that will gradually disperse more and more of the 100 trillion dollars every year is a more realistic combination of "trickle down" and "rise-up" economics. The challenge is to ensure the money is dispersed among communities in need, philanthropies, displaced workers, essential workers and lower level employees at first. After a system like this is normalized, the next stage can more easily place a focus on meeting the basic needs of humans on a global scale. It is possible to do with existing technology and the right amount of demand and oversight from customer and stakeholder advocates.

Those who earn $6 million or more annually should not be vilified. These are the folks who played a major role in building modern society. That is not meant to diminish the blood, sweat and tears of the billions of people who earn less than $6 million per year. The few who do earn multi-millions likely make big decisions and spend big money in ways that have altered directly or indirectly, accidentally or purposefully the way we live. Arguably, the majority of those decisions and expenditures have been made with good intentions, and the results have seemed great for the most part. Overall the world is getting better and more peaceful. We live in a time of god-like technologies, endless entertainment, breathtaking structures, incredible infrastructure—and so much more. Much of it has been created by people and organizations with big money.

How much a person "earns" can be difficult to measure if you include executive perks, investments, benefits, offshore accounts, etc. The idea here is to set measurable goals in simple, plausible terms to gain traction with the greatest number of people. By year 2030, the economists, politicians and regulators will have to work out the specifics. No matter what, regulation and tax laws always have loopholes, and many wealthy people and businesses will legally find and use those loopholes. When the loopholes get filled, new loopholes open up...it is never ending. If you believe human suffering can be reduced by redistribution of extreme wealth, then we need a starting point to get the wheels in motion on an income cap.

Like the founding fathers of the United States, these early 21ˢᵗ century people of great wealth are the grandparents of modern-day society. Now doesn't that have a nice ring to it? Better than "the 1%." Appropriately, these matriarchs and patriarchs of the beautiful world we get to enjoy are grandfathered (appropriate term!) into their financial status. In the near future, perhaps we can see what sort of world the masses create with more hope, more resources and fewer financial burdens.

HOW DO WE GET FROM HERE TO THERE?

How do we redefine the constructs of our world? It's already happening. There's a revolution afoot within all constructs whether you personally change or not. The important question is:

"What can I do to ensure this transformation is beneficial for me?"

Awareness is step one. Action is step two. By the end of this book you will have the tools to accomplish both.

Something we can all do right away is evaluate the message we send to businesses—essentially vote with our dollars. We are concentrating our collective money into certain sectors. As I write this, healthcare, technology and construction are some of the largest industries. The largest conglomerates in which personal expenditures cluster include banks, insurance, and pharmaceutical companies. The money left over in our **personal budgets** is spread thin; just like our time.

Interesting to note: if you think a huge concentration of wealth in certain industries means they have a huge responsibility to properly govern those funds; then consider that you, too, have a huge responsibility if you live in the States because U.S. citizens hold the largest concentration of the wealth in the world. Therefore you actually wield great power in determining how money in the world is distributed.

Every time you make a purchase with a credit card or any digital form, with every single click on a computer, every "like" or "follow," every online search, even every place you go you generate DATA. Once the information is tracked, it is assembled to create a digital representation of you and your behaviors, then sold for fractions of a cent in milliseconds to various media outlets, and any business or other organization, including governmental ones that use consumer or citizen behavior patterns to inform their production and distribution strategies. The idea is to make your experience as customized and tailored to your behaviors, wants and needs as possible.

If you commit to The Alpha Bet in your everyday life, you will shift the data you feed all the tracking technologies.

Say you begin to **demonstrate** a focus on health by using frequently a fitness app you've downloaded on your phone. Next the location service on your phone tracks your visits to a homeless shelter once per week. Plus you end up writing off more taxes at the end of the year with charitable expenses. Then you address your buying habits, shifting your personal **demand** for products to Green Certification[9] choices rather than just brand names; and while you're at it you begin to buy fewer products and look for more service-based companies. Online, you bookmark and visit regularly sites like World Economic Forum, and you use the "Ecosia" search engine to find some of the terminology in this book. Eventually you are ready to **declutter** and so you go to www.consumer.ftc.gov and search for "stopping-unsolicited-mail-phone-calls-and-email" to opt out of solicitations. You think about how to reduce and reuse more in your life, and begin with taking measures to reduce your monthly energy and water bills. Finally, you want to reduce your fuel expense, so you talk to your boss and she agrees to let you work twice per week from home.

The above are all easy stage one "gateway goodness". Simple changes like these will start to snowball into more goodness in your life, because the constructs, which are more and more governed by data and algorithms, will see how you are changing. Others will follow, because that's

---

9   Any number of certifications for social responsibility and particularly environmental sustainability. See examples at www.3talliance.org/certs.

what humans do (i.e. Social Proofing[10]) but also because the algorithms know who you communicate with and will send subtle suggestions to them as well...such as an advertisement for an eco-friendly product. Imagine if everyone started shifting their behaviors. We have the power to rethink the systematic cycles we have become accustomed to, but which do not necessarily keep us happy.

Products and services are designed for a continuous cycle of consumption. The basic idea from the consumer point of view today is:

> I make money by working on stuff that people can buy. I use that money to buy stuff that other people make. All this stuff needs to be replaced at some point, and so I need to keep making money.

And from the business point of view:

> Businesses extract materials from earth, manufacture a product, sell the product to a consumer for money, and then the consumer must discard the product at some point so that the business can keep receiving more money.

It doesn't have to be this way any longer. Machines and robotics can create stuff that may never need to be repaired in your lifetime. This creates a challenge that most economists can't get over.... How do I afford stuff, if I'm not

---

10 (a.k.a. behavioral contagion) Is a psychological phenomenon where people assume the actions of others in an attempt to reflect correct behavior for a given situation. Typically an instinctual decision rather than a conscious decision.

working as much and earning money to produce stuff? One answer is more social capital for the people and less profit incentives for the businesses.

Globalization 4.0 will birth the rise of greater SOCIAL CAPITAL acceptance and the beginning of the end for PROFIT. What is profit really? What happens with it? There is no standardized rule on how to use profit. There never has been. To be a bit simplistic, this is what businesses usually use profit for:
- Capital expenditures
- Research and development
- Executive bonuses or stock options
- Shareholder dividends
- Other investments/businesses/acquisitions to grow the money
- Interest, taxes, and insurance
- Becoming self-insured
- Paying off debts
- Savings for rainy days

Hundreds of billions of dollars will continue to be managed by the whims and strategies of the largest corporations in the world, and will stay mostly concentrated in the upper echelons of society and sitting in derivatives, unless governments and consumers mandate that some of the profit must be distributed to meet societal needs and environmental protections.

As a business guiding light and prevailing metric, does profit lead to manipulation of our consumer behaviors?

Does the pursuit of profit cause excessive production of **things** we may not necessarily need...things that degrade the environment along the supply chain, and eventually end up cluttering our lives?

KNOW WHAT YOU STAND FOR

Before we embark upon new economic measures and a new structure for the way we live, work and consume, it is important that we remember to teach the Alpha Generation to embody the time-tested values common among many religions, cultures, and philosophies. Here are the 12 predominate values the Alpha Agreement aims to emulate, on the following page.

TWELVE ALPHA VALUES

Find the calm when there is chaos. There is a bigger picture. **SELF-CONTROL**

You will be challenged, and you will fail sometimes, but keep trying. **PERSEVERANCE**

Those who make mistakes or have a bad day deserve mercy. Practice empathy. **FOREGIVENESS**

People are happy around you, because of your positive presence. **HAPPINESS**

You are not a cog in a wheel. You are unique and should explore our diverse world. **VARIETY**

Appreciate altruists, and those who are virtuous. Always be a warrior for good. **LOYALTY**

Always try to do the right thing. Fight your fears and any compulsive vice. **COURAGE**

People trust you because you are honest. Speak your truth and be vulnerable. **TRUTH**

Find opportunities to share your talents. Be generous and demonstrate kindness often. **LOVE**

Be your best self; maintain your system and take time to recharge. **HEALTH**

No need to worry; simply slow down at times and enjoy every minute. **PATIENCE**

Seek viewpoints that are different from yours. Collaborate with others and truly listen. **RESPECT**

We know the difference between right and wrong, but we are far from perfect beings. The Alpha Bet puts the pressure on the Alpha Gen to create morally perfect technologies. The Alpha Gen will be building on our revision of the constructs around us, and if we draw the maps they can outperform us in short order.

If we take The Alpha Bet, we commit to altering the way we interact with social networks, economic systems, and political frameworks that still use 20th century methods.

Consciously, or not, most people in the world are betting on scientists, experts and ultimately the Alpha Gen to grow up and fix societal, inequality, and environmental problems. The more people are aware of the constructs and our power to alter them, the more powerful the transformation becomes. Technologies will rule more and more the way we live, work and consume as we enter the era of Globalization 4.0. You will excel in the following decade if you live your values and if you challenge prevailing theories of how people should spend their money and time.

CHAPTER IV

2020 THEORY

"THE THEORY IS THAT YEAR 2020 WAS THE MOMENT WHEN MACHINES GOT 'SMART,' AND WE NOW HAVE THE CHOICE TO TEACH THEM TO PERPETUATE HUMAN KINDNESS, MODERATION, AND SYMBIOSIS WITH NATURE; OR TO TEACH THEM TO MAKE MATERIAL EXCESS A PRIORITY."

ꟼI⅃Ⅎ NOISIⱯ

Out with the old FIXED MINDSET.
In with the new GROWTH MINDSET.

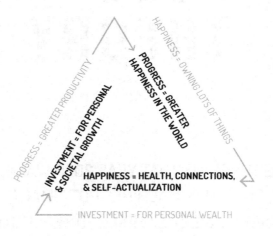

Revolution is happening right under our noses. You can feel it, right? It's not a big conspiracy or a plan at all. It is a natural transformation. Big changes are happening, but we are accidentally allowing some of the problems of the past to persist and grow stronger as well. To get ahead, we must acknowledge this transformation and shift our personal life script.

Virtually every futurist, every data scientist knows what is about to happen. They've seen (and drawn) multiple trajectory charts that show the growth of Emerging Technologies and exponential innovation. The next stage is lower costs, easier access and wider acceptance. So how can we effectively use all this knowledge and the cool new affordable tech?

This is where 2020 Theory comes in. It is a three-stage approach to changing the world. The genesis is that year 2020 was the moment when machines got "smart," and we now have the choice to teach them to perpetuate human kindness, moderation, and symbiosis with nature; or instead to teach them to make material excess a priority.

2020 Theory begins with four basic assumptions:
1. Humanity is on a path of self-destruction but it's not too late to course correct.
2. The human drive to innovate and progress should not and cannot be stopped, it can only be stalled.
3. There will always be extreme views for and against any new idea. We must carefully embrace new ideas but find a compromise to allow opposing forces to tug and pull in balance.
4. Most humans must undergo stages of experiential failure in order to accept that actionable change is necessary. So, we cannot skip pain and failure as a society, but we can plan for it, mitigate, and safeguard the desired results.

STAGE ONE: THE ALPHA BET
Altering individual behaviors.

Stage One begins before year 2030, but after individuals have the ability to mobilize (peacefully) on a global scale, such as 80% or more of people on Earth having access to the internet. Stage One is about working within the boundaries of our current systems and constructs.

The objective is to challenge people to consciously change their normal routine and take action to change the world. Specifically examining personal perceptions, finances, lifestyles, surroundings, workplaces, and citizenship behaviors in a way that diverges from 20th century concepts. The primary purpose is to break the old constructs and influence observational artificial intelligence technologies (such as business marketing, intelligence, and analytics A.I. software) to adapt its algorithms accordingly.

The three "D"s to start changing the world is DEMAND (such as at retailers, on social media, and at work); DECLUTTER (such as reducing waste, blocking advertisements, and spending less on new products); and DEMONSTRATE (such as contacting leaders as a united front, volunteering more, and making wellness a priority). If 20% of consumer behaviors shift toward equitable and sustainable purchases, then businesses and governments will begin to adapt.

Toward the end of Stage One, philanthropic causes will have greater financial and human capital; however, it will become apparent nonprofit systems need to be repaired with increased virtual volunteering, administrative restructuring and supply chain improvements. Specifically, nonprofits catering to the reconstructing of health, food distribution, affordable housing and education models will need the greatest concentration of efforts as many antiquated societal constructs continue to fail. These nonprofit oriented support programs will need to be tailored to the individual with a preventative and long-term sustainable strategy.

A key component in the transition to Stage Two is when consumer pressure causes the majority of for-profit businesses to halve their environmental impact, their profits, marketing budgets, and executive pay scales. These behavior changes will have to begin with bold early adopters among consumers and businesses (one Harvard study found that societal change often occurs after just 3.5% of a population leads the way).

STAGE TWO: HINDSIGHT 2020

Building new institutional constructs.

Stage Two could begin before year 2040, but after enterprise, economics, and governance models break due to a global scale catastrophe such as a pandemic, pervasive environmental disasters, inequalities reaching critical mass, automations eliminating more jobs than creating new ones, or a combination of massive disruptions.

Year 2020 was the year everyone in the world felt the cracks in our institutional constructs. It's a natural entropy; these systems will continue to breakdown, but new solutions will gain traction. Particularly, Virtual Nations (V.N.) will arise offering guaranteed basic needs. These V.N.s will essentially be online groups utilizing currencies such as "Proof of Stake blockchain" for greater Social Capital (or smart phone distributed blockchain social capital). Many of the major social media platforms are positioned to evolve into effective V.N. systems. True V.N.s must be not-for-profit. Its governance can be augmented with artificial intelligence and includes ways to participate as a citizen, such as voting tokens for establishing policies and rules. Some current day V.N.s include: Bitnation, Asgardia, Sovereign Peace, The Good Country, and Republic of Estonia.

The general ethos for this Stage Two rebuilding period must be biomimicry, digital security and ethical automation. This is a time to increase technology usage, meanwhile taking the time to audit everything to ensure things like implicit bias, cyber threats and profit-as-purpose motives are removed from any system. A.I. with quantum computing power will be available to assist.

Toward the end of Stage Two, extreme poverty will be eliminated. Democracies will emerge where people truly have the power (rather than plutocracies or corporatocracies in which wealth and businesses hold the power). Some countries will be governed by technology as in a A.I. noocracy or technocracy.

A key component in the transition to Stage Three is an agreement between nation states to congruously and multilaterally reduce military might. The purpose will be to transition those funds to ensure maintainable health, education and infrastructure improvements at home, and afar in places prone to crime, suffering or war.

The only way to transition to Stage Three is a general higher level of empathy and consciousness brought about by medical breakthroughs, along with noninvasive brain-computer-interface technology. These technologies will have to be as globally acceptable, inexpensive and widely used as smartphones. Altering the human condition with technology has never been an ideal solution, but we will reach the point when we must choose to evolve, hide, or die.

STAGE THREE: ENTER THE FRINJA
Refine with gamification.

Stage Three could begin before year 2050, but after planetary resources are fully measured, managed and sustainable for all life on Earth.

The objective is to examine what we've learned from the massive transformations that have taken place during Stages One and Two, then streamline with "first principles thinking." The focus is on reducing complexities and maximizing resource regeneration (such as mastering zero-point energy[1]).

At this stage, every person will have their basic needs met and environmental adversities will be under control. Global debts between nations will become a "sunk cost" and will only weigh down human progress. Economics and politics will be so intertwined and interdependent across the globe that human progress becomes a shared effort. Financial debts and business proprietary rights become a thing of the past. Every business tool and method is open sourced in order to achieve the most efficient and highest quality products and services for every human. Banks will become artificial intelligence hubs, storing data and managing energy distribution.

Money and property will no longer be top of mind, but there will be new issues to contend with. There will be too

---

1   The lowest possible energy that a quantum mechanical system may have. Harnessing this energy would mean generating power from the moving molecules, protons, electrons, neutrons, or dark matter within anything (air, object, or being).

much dependence on technology, and we must quickly scale back where possible. Transhumanism[2] will cause a rift in society. People will live longer, happier and healthier lives; but we must consider what are the consequences if we "cure" aging?

Overall, life on Earth will be better than ever in Stage Three. Everyone in the world will be invited to take part in an experiential gamified method to create the future to get input from multiple experiences, and "multiple intelligences." A set of Artificial General Intelligence machines will aggregate the data from the human input to help define and augment a new social contract as the foundation for the new societal constructs that maintain global peace and balance. Ideas from the mainstream, to the regressive, to the progressive, all the way to the fringe will be important in refining the path forward. This is the end of the Anthropocene Epoch as we transition to a Civilization Type One (CT1)[3].

Entertainment will rule many people's lives and the ethics of various new forms of entertainment will often be challenged. A key component of Stage Three will be an existential threat of World War between all "good" A.I. and all

---

2   The use of sophisticated technologies to enhance human intellect and physiology (such as human augmentation with brain-computer-interfaces, nano-medication, and designer gene therapy).

3   A civilization which has mastered and can fully control its planetary energy, information and resources in a way that provides for continued regeneration and distribution systems that support an ever-improving lived experience for all of its inhabitants while managing and mitigating any existential threats. Other theories on Civilization Type One have been proposed by the World Future Society, the Venus Project, Game B, Carl Sagan, and the Kardashev Scale.

"bad" A.I. Humanity as a whole must join forces and band together against a common enemy in order to survive.

Near the end of Stage Three, prior to CT1, we will be systematizing the ethical policies, politics and economics of two imminent evolutions: the advancement of artificial super intelligence, and also terraforming other planets.

Back to Earth for now. The following is a 2020 Theory stage one tool for you, me, or any individual to directly take agency in changing the world for the better. This is a guide to get started thinking about the goals you can accomplish in life, one at a time, by connecting your RESOURCES to the CHANGES that are taking place around you.

THE THREE CONCENTRATIONS

PEOPLE: educate, inform and conduct awareness changes within communities.
BUSINESS: produce organizational changes and overall economic activity.
GOVERNMENT: set up global systems, connections and interrelation processes.

The three concentration areas above lay the groundwork. The Vision, Mission and Values of 2020 Theory follow.

2020 VISION

Humanity has reached a critical crossroad. In today's world we each take more than what deeply sustains us. We can now harness the peak of our collective intellect, empathy and capacity for technological innovation to build a global society that continues to respect individuality but in balance with nature and each other.

2020 MISSION

2020 Theory is based on the idea that we can make greater progress as humans if we examine how we define our own progress and evolve accordingly. 2020 Theory is the moment of reflection and reinvention we must each take to live happier, more intentional lives. If we all take action together, we can collectively improve the world around us.

2020 VALUES

2020 Theory leads to definitive action when we internalize and act on the following beliefs:

- We believe human progress can be measured in happiness and the positive impact we make on the world around us.
- We believe happiness is defined as the ability of all people on Earth to have the intellectual and financial freedom to be healthy, to pursue their passion and to participate in a supportive community.
- We believe that this freedom can be built through dedicated and aligned long-term investment in

personal, professional, societal and governmental growth.

- We believe if we all participate in 2020 Theory, the result will be massively improved lifestyle, business and government practices that respect our time, each other and the world we live in.

COMPONENTS OF 2020 THEORY

Select three Pillars of **Change** below: one from the Constructs, one from the Tools, and one from the Objectives. Next, select just one of the Individual **Resources** that you believe can be used to help transform the Pillar of Change. Then choose a 2020 Theory **Tenet** and one **Obstacle** to beware of. Finally consider how you can apply all of this to achieve one of the 2020 Theory **Goals**.

Or if you are into mathematical formulas, 2020 Theory may look something like this:

$$x = \frac{\Delta a + \Delta b + \Delta c}{[r\,(\mathrm{t})] - o}$$

PILLARS OF CHANGE

(Δa)   **Global Constructs** (operational resources/institutions) are changing their methods.
Community (and individuals), Businesses, and Governments.

(Δb)   **Global Tools** (Exponential Power of transformative technologies) accelerating.
Automation & Artificial Intelligence (RPAs & A.I.s), Other Emerging Technologies (EmTech), and Globalization.

(Δc)   **Global Objectives** (Desired Goals, Responsibilities & Purpose) are becoming more clear.
Economics revised, Environment healthier, and Society happier.

INDIVIDUAL RESOURCES (r)

Time: Outsource and understand value of your time.

Abundance Planning: Meditation, Design thinking, Systems thinking, Exponential thinking, Making, Governing the Commons, Reframing, and Storytelling.

Experiential Learning: Kinesthetic, video, and audio methods. Learning how to learn all life long, as well as compassion, focus/presence and emotional intelligence.

Technology: Internet, online reviews and feedback, 3D printing, A.I., etc.

Network (local and global): Collaboration; and forming new and diverse relationships.

Money: Natural capital, social capital, cryptotokens, alternate currencies, and general consumer spending power.

2020 THEORY TENETS (*t*)

Perception: Perception is everything. All humans are connected. Challenge preconceptions. Stop and look around. Are you in the right spot, or is it time to course correct? Wake up and see with 20/20 clarity.

Lifestyle: Evolve. Practice common sense, and don't act on feelings of fear, revenge and greed. Search for a new path. Don't follow the trodden trail of those before you. You are a Superbeing compared to all other humans in history. We're capable of so much more.

Work: Harness the innovative energy around you. Be innovative and open to new ideas. Be open to uncomfortable ideas...use the momentum of innovation to your advantage.

Finances: Follow the time. Wealth is time, not things. Be stealthy wealthy: consume less, live more...work less, play more.

Surroundings: Goodness exponentiates. Embrace change and seek opportunities to help others. Take time to help the Earth and also other humans along the way. It will make your journey better.

Citizenship: Light the way. Be vulnerable and speak out. Behave in a way that aligns with your values.

OBSTACLES TO BEWARE OF (*o*)

Preconceptions: Old school concepts die hard, and misinformation sharing is rampant. What beliefs have your parents, teachers, or community held true that may need reconsidering?

Primal instincts: Fear, revenge and greed are often unsubstantiated in a world with so much abundance. Your life has greater purpose when you respect others and contribute to the greater good. Where is there an opportunity in your life to develop your 6th sense...common sense?

Work ethic meaning of life: You're taught to study hard then strive for a lucrative career, so that one day you can retire and live out the end of your days however you choose. Is your true purpose in life to make as much money as possible? If you had more personal time to flex your "creativity muscles," what would you attempt to do?

Blindness to marketing tactics: The root of many financial problems boils down to excessive ADVERTISING. What would the world look like in the absence of advertising?

Resisting change: Should we resist new technologies if they threaten a human job sector? Historically, there is no stopping progress, only stalling it. Should humans even be working in a job that is so mundane that a software or robot could do it better?

Feelings of powerlessness: Your weakness is in your head. In order to grow and learn, we must be ourselves and we must make mistakes, fail, and press on. Vulnerability is opportunity. An invitation to reach a new level of confidence. What is a situation where you have felt vulnerable? If you are respectful of others, then what is the worst thing that will happen if you speak and live your truth?

2020 THEORY GOALS (x)

Health: More time for healthy activities. Less manipulation of your time and psyche. Higher priority of physical, mental, spiritual and/or emotional exercise. And healthier environment.

Happiness: Helping others. More common sense. Simplicity (reduced clutter/waste & time wastes). Daily gratitude. More truth recognized and expressed. And fewer worries.

Community & Family Connections: Tighter-knit community and family. Time to be in the moment with those who matter most to you (in person). And collaborate with others, be inclusive and network with diverse groups.

Guaranteed Basic Needs: Not because everyone deserves it, but because we can. For the first time in history, we have the tools to make this happen, and end much suffering, while opening the door to more opportunity. Social Capital incentives to volunteer more. Shift your focus from survival to self-actualization. Clarity and more mental bandwidth. And less suffering in the world.

Safety: Human rights protected and more widely accepted as rights of each human on Earth. Reduced threat of crime (cyber/physical/other), terrorism, and natural disasters. Better insulation from those same potential threats. Technologies built ethically (especially A.I.). And better platforms to give feedback.

Achievement: Flexible work schedule. Spend more time on a passion. Cultural values directed away from accumulation of money and things. Identify, share and monetize your talents. Time, resources and opportunity to be creative/innovative. Time, resources and opportunity to learn new things. Time, resources and opportunity to exchange talents.

HOW TO APPLY 2020 THEORY

In order to focus the philosophy of 2020 Theory into one area of transformation in your life, fill this out:

If the construct of _____ Δa _____

can add the tool of _____ Δb _____

with the objective of making _____ Δc _____;

and if I can multiply the _____ t _____ tenet

within my _____ r _____ resources

and subtract _____ o _____ as an obstacle;

then there is opportunity in reconsidering how I divide my Resources among the Constructs around me in order to cultivate an improved _____ x _____ goal.

For example, your 2020 Theory formula could be something like this:

If the construct of **Businesses**

can add the tool of **Globalization**

with the objective of making **Society Happier**;

and if I can multiply the **Perception** tenet

within my local **Network** resources

and subtract **Feelings of Powerlessness** as an obstacle;

then there is opportunity in reconsidering how I divide my Resources among the Constructs around me in order to cultivate an improved **Guaranteed Basic Needs** goal.

The method to the madness is each person can interpret their 2020 Theory as they see fit. And keep in mind, this is just a starting point. You may find to achieve an even better solution you can use multiple resources, tools, and so forth.

The above formula can be interpreted as a mission to ask your friends and family to help come up with ways your place of work can help bring access to healthy meals to anyone in the world. If you feel like your friends and family, your place of work, and the basic needs of people in other countries have nothing to do with each other, then perhaps that's just your feeling of powerlessness creeping in. Get creative and be bold.

Infinite opportunities to make the world a better place exist. The theory is you WILL find a specific opportunity that only you will come up with, because your capabilities and frame of reference are unique to you...as long as you begin to explore the issues, begin to connect the dots, and then execute on your idea.

In this random scenario above, maybe your place of work has a materials supplier overseas and this supplier provides materials to grocery stores and restaurants all over the world, as well. During your research you realize a friend knows the manager at a grocery store, and you find the grocery store throws out 20% of its produce due to over-stocking and food spoilage.

Pretend this is your scenario: do you know anyone in your local networks who works with food or another basic need such as water, clothing or shelter? What are your thoughts on how to prevent food spoilage in this scenario, how to repurpose the old produce, or how to get it to people in need before it spoils?

If the tool for this scenario is **Automation & Artificial Intelligence**, you may come up with a result such as a machine to measure the ripeness of the produce on the shelf, or a method of tracking consumer behaviors to maximize ordering efficiency, or a grocery delivery service that also picks up old food waste for composting. If the tool is **EmTech** (other than RPA and A.I.), then you could come up with a process to grow cultured meat with cellular agriculture in "food deserts," or to create 3D printed treats with old produce before it spoils, or to develop an Augmented Reality (AR)[4] app for customers to hold up their phone camera to the produce to determine the age and avoid waste at home.

But for this scenario we have selected **Globalization** and so you may find the local grocery store will give you their old produce free, and you experiment with honey and chia seeds to make a healthy jam. You video the process on YouTube and ask your materials supplier at work to send the video to all of their restaurants and grocery store contacts.

In order to execute on any idea, you need to first brainstorm on possible unintended consequences, and then simply share the refined idea with someone who can make it a reality. You may even identify an income opportunity for yourself during the process and choose to get some crowdfunding to start up a business around your idea.

---

4   An overlay of computer-generated content on the real world that can superficially interact with the environment in real-time.

HUMAN THINKING IS A PARADOX

Convincing ourselves to execute on the idea, no matter how simple, is difficult. If you don't follow through, then everything remains the same. If you do take a leap of faith, then you have just cracked the reality that feels safe, but may not be the best reality for you. The CHANGE you have been looking for might fall into your lap, but only if you take action to trigger that change. Our instincts resist change, but our minds desire change. Follow your heart, follow what you know is right. Our instincts are designed to adapt. Our instincts will follow our actions, guaranteed. It just takes persistence and a little practice.

> *It is a time when one's spirit is subdued and sad, one knows not why; when the past seems a storm-swept desolation, life a vanity and a burden, and the future but a way to death. It is a time when one is filled with vague longings; when one dreams of flight to peaceful islands in the remote solitudes of the sea, or folds his hands and says," What is the use of struggling, and toiling and worrying any more? Let us give it all up.*

This is what Mark Twain said about the end of the 19th century in his book *The Gilded Age*. The world today still has serious social problems masked by a gilding of material excess. We have a tremendous abundance of stuff, but extreme poverty and suffering simultaneously. Across the globe, people, institutions and societies deal with social and environmental challenges, each highly dependent on local characteristics, cultures, values and perceptions. Those of us living in countries where communication is constant and comprehensive, hear about some of the challenges from one or another news source, and then we quickly forget and go back to our routines.

Usually we see problems and look the other way, excusing ourselves with arguments such as:

There are others already working to solve the problems, and they're better equipped than I am.
This doesn't seem to affect my life.
I have more pressing problems of my own.
The situation is beyond my control.

Yes, these seem to be legitimate reasons. It may only be those special people who fight their excuses who actually cause change in the world. Today being a passive citizen hands over more power than ever to profit-motivated entities. Today more than ever, we must practice challenging our excuses. If we don't, our excuse-making mentality will create for more and more people a painfully boring existence in which resources dwindle and anxieties increase. What you do and what you choose not to do will affect the world in one way or another, and as unlikely as it may seem, those effects will reach people and places you may not even be familiar with.

The 2020 Theory can be used to find realistic, simple actions YOU can take to change the world. You now have a plan in your hands. Perhaps only a select few will see these words, will read what's written here, but many more can and will change based on what you choose to do after today. We tend to do what those around us are doing. Let's take advantage of this to steadily infuse change until it becomes universal.

There will be some sacrifices, but these are only temporary. Stage One of the 2020 Theory is a 10-year dedication to set the path of humanity on the right trajectory. After 2030, we can take a big collective sigh of relief and enjoy the new world together with the 1%, with regular folk of all demographics, and with superhero Change Agents of the future like you. It may seem we are attacking big business, Big Brother and the 1%, but that is not the intention. This disparity needs to be addressed, because it is an evident top-of-mind concern for many people in the world who are fortunate enough to be concerned about things larger than meeting their basic needs.

Still, it is only one piece of a much larger puzzle. It is important for everyone to understand that big business, Big Brother and the 1% also donate the majority of funds supporting charities at large. Thus far, they have been great saviors of our way of life and our ever-improving humanity. Without the kindness and philanthropic giving of athletes, celebrities, big businesses and high-level executives, the worldwide situation would be much more dire than it is today.

Our way of life is changing; therefore, "business as usual" must change as well. Business As Usual (also known as: BAU) implies a focus of increasing profit margins with little regard to social or environmental impact. It's a system that fosters mounting inequalities the longer it goes on... until it eventually breaks, there's a revolution, or the system massively changes its BAU.

We consumers are starting to feel the societal and environmental consequences of a hundred years of what has been BAU. For example, due to climate change, more people are seeking products and services that are ecologically friendly and so BAU must adapt. If businesses continue BAU, they will soon begin to feel the pain of resource depletion and higher costs due to material scarcity. Globalization is also affecting our way of life because we can directly buy from and sell to anyone in the world. BAU must change as the landscape of global competition and interdependence continues to affect local markets. Technology is one of the most obvious drivers of change in our lives that necessitates BAU to evolve. In our life today, we expect to get what we want fast and tailored to our personal liking. Due to a plethora of options and advertisements in our lives, our attention is scarce.

Businesses will need a new "usual" that factors in stakeholder health and social capital to effectively build networks and garner community support. Automation (and pandemic risks) will cause more workers to turn to gig-work and WFH (Work From Home) jobs. In the short-term, this will decrease consumer discretionary spending on the whole, may disrupt the banking industry, and will require businesses to focus more on **essential** products and services.

What products and services are essential in your 21st century lifestyle? How could these essential products and services change within 10 years? As demand increases for the essentials, the innovations and the costs will become more abundant and more affordable. Consider advancements and cost reductions in video conferencing, virtual reality, drone delivery, 3D printing, robotic home maintenance, Personal Protective Equipment (PPE), and so on. What have we learned from the 2020 pandemic? In what ways do you think Business As Usual should change?

SOCIAL CAPITAL SYSTEMS

In the next 10 years, Social Capital can give more opportunity and power to the people. It will play an increasingly significant role in transforming the world. Martin Luther King, Jr. spoke truth and common sense. One of his concerns (that still needs to be addressed today) is how to restructure our societal constructs so that they do not produce beggars. A famous quote of his from 1967 is,

We must rapidly begin the shift from a "thing-oriented" society to a "person-oriented" society. When machines and computers, profit motives and property rights are considered more important than people, the giant triplets of racism, materialism, and militarism are incapable of being conquered.

We need to carefully craft the future now, before technologies developed for the advancement of one owner, one group, one ideology instead of for the common good do

87

it for us later. We're all in this together. The golden rule is more than a rule; it is a law of nature. You will be treated as you treat others, especially if you learn to treat them as they want to be treated. The world will respond to you in the same manner you treat the world around you.

Social Capital is one method to begin measuring a lot more than Gross Domestic Product (GDP) as the major national success metric. Imagine a world in which we measure and incentivize true Human Progress Indicators, rather than metrics and incentives tied to money.

A Social Capital system is one way to tip the scales of inequality slightly back into balance, so long as it is limited in scope to incentivize specific activities that are considered good for society. To start, Citizen Social Capital points can be calculated with an app or online tool managed by a nonprofit. The weight of Social Capital points can change depending on how much need there is in certain areas measured by Human Progress Indicators.

Some examples of ways to earn Social Capital points:

- Volunteering personal data (such as genealogical data, online behavior, or epidemiological tracing)
- Loaning money to others interest free
- Attending an annual physical exam
- Improving or maintaining a healthy BMI
- Becoming a community representative[5]
- Volunteering in times of crisis or disaster
- Volunteering in general
- Voting

And, spending your Social Capital points could be limited to help pay for certain needs, rather than using it like cash for products and services that are not identified as providing the most good for society. Examples include:

- Education
- Healthcare
- Housing
- Utilities
- Transportation
- Internet access
- Insurance
- Items or service from businesses ranking high in Social Capital scores

---

5   The plan to have trained health and security professionals who live in each community in the U.S. as a resource and a preventative measure to identify community security or individual health issues proactively. One proposed format is a collaboration between social workers, police, USPS workers, and delivery people. For details, visit www.3talliance.org/reps.

Each form of granted Social Capital can have a base amount issued annually as cryptocurrency to each participant. The goal is to eventually allow every citizen to earn more toward a decentralized Social Capital bank account in exchange for activities such as maintaining a healthy lifestyle, volunteering, or anything else deemed good for society within an individual's particular capability. A Social Capital tracking app like this can be developed by a nonprofit, but ultimately the power of the Social Capital points could be amplified if the government backs the idea and its implementation. On a local, city or state level, this could be achieved more easily and proven before federal adoption. In the short-term, governments will have to institute a tax hike to cover some of the costs, along with business regulation to ensure companies that automate away human jobs are utilizing their newfound profit, capabilities and resources to help basic need services to become more cost efficient.

A democratized government-sponsored Social Capital system could eventually pay for itself by PROACTIVELY improving the health and resources of its people...consequently reducing the high cost of crime and illness. Most social services receiving federal funding can seamlessly tie into the framework of Social Capital. For example, the following services can all be replaced and streamlined into the Citizen Social Capital currency: Social Security, Medicare, Medicaid, SNAP food benefits, Supplemental Security Income, agricultural subsidies, housing subsidies, TANF welfare, Head Start, and childcare aid.

Note: China has created a Social Credit system for its citizens which some say goes too far in capturing personal data. Purportedly, a citizen's social score in China can go up or down even based on with whom that person's family members associate. Perhaps a simpler system that rewards socially responsible behavior is worth exploring, but with some added constraints such as far less government control and more citizen control on a blockchain. What do you think a universally acceptable Social Capital system could look like?

100 YEARS OF CHANGE

Picture life in the year 1986. What if a book had come out that predicted by year 2020 you would be recording "reality" TV shows and downloading commercial-free movies to your TV without the need to rewind for the next person to watch. You'll pay your bills and handle your banking "online" with a small phone-computer. You could drive a car that runs on only battery power. And you'll get in cars with strangers (Uber) and stay at other strangers' homes (AirBnB).

Explaining smart phones to someone in 1986 would have made them think the 21st century would be a Utopian Shangri-La. Nearly everyone would have a handheld device with the knowledge of the world on it, plus the capability to show a satellite image of exactly where they're standing and send a message to anyone in the world instantly. This device could play just about any song ever recorded. It will also record and save virtually unlimited videos and take clear, high-definition photos to share instantly with friends and family and strangers. In the year 1986, you would have said:

"MAYBE ALL THAT COULD HAPPEN IN A HUNDRED YEARS. YOU'VE BEEN WATCHING TOO MUCH STAR TREK OR THE JETSONS."

It happened almost overnight and our stress levels and excessive work habits didn't change at all. Some people claim our collective stress and work levels have actually increased. It is not a Utopia, but we do have much more "abundance" in general. We are just now learning how to manage it.

Technology is moving faster and becoming smaller and smarter by the day. Just a few years ago, you would have questioned if driverless cars could ever be a reality, but now your view has changed.

The 2020 Theory is not extreme. It is intentionally kept very tangible and relevant to fit into your current lifestyle. This way, those who join us can drop out at any time when it begins to feel too sci-fi. At this point, the future possibilities seem distant to anyone who has not researched what is happening particularly in the fields of A.I. and Biology.

Major innovations and discoveries are occurring daily. The only thing slowing progress is how quickly humans can connect the dots, along with the fact that at the same time profit motives smother new discoveries in proprietary quicksand.

The few born in 1920 who have lived to be 100 years old have seen an incredible shift in the way we think and the way we live. For example, in 1920 astronomers believed there was nothing outside of the Milky Way galaxy...just empty space. Now consider the generation born in 2020. What will they see in **2120**? At this point many of us believe the human body cannot live forever, time follows a linear path, there is nothing bigger than the universe and it probably started with a big bang, there is nothing smaller than a quark, most plants and animals aren't very intelligent, the weather and natural disasters cannot be controlled, and energy is only derived from a few sources like solar, wind, nuclear, heat, and water. What do we place a limit on today, that may in fact be much more expansive than we can see through the present filter of knowledge?

The filters through which we have seen the world for the past century are breaking. The philosophy of the 2020 Theory will help you become an active participant in this transformation rather than a bystander. The Alpha Gen will likely continue to evolve and transform the world long after your time spent as a change agent. But the changes you make in your life in the 2020s will help build a strong foundational framework for the Alpha Gen moving forward.

TRANSFORM LIFESTYLE
Let us travel beyond the limits of those before us.
We shall take chances and be prepared for a new adventure
embracing a more mindful routine and abandoning
feelings of fear, revenge and greed.

CHAPTER V

PERCEPTION FLIPPING

"WE FEEL GREATER INNER PEACE
WHEN WE UNTANGLE THE PERCEPTION
OF OUR OWN NEEDS AND DESIRES BY
CONNECTING THEM TO LARGER SOCIETAL
IMPACTS OUTSIDE OF OURSELVES."

∀ISION FLIP

Out with the old FIXED MINDSET.
In with the new GROWTH MINDSET.

PLANET CHANGING—AND
INNOVATIVE SOLUTIONS ABOUND

SOCIETY CRUMBLING

MASSIVE SOCIAL INVESTMENT—
ESPECIALLY FROM THE 1%

PLANET DYING

LESS HUMAN SUFFERING—
THAN EVER BEFORE GLOBALLY

MONEY SILOED IN THE 1%

"MAN SACRIFICES HIS HEALTH IN ORDER
TO MAKE MONEY. THEN HE SACRIFICES
MONEY TO RECUPERATE HIS HEALTH."

-DALAI LAMA

Humans are preprogrammed to spend a lot of time
thinking about themselves. Ironically, we feel greater inner

peace when we untangle the perception of our own **needs and desires** by connecting them to larger societal impacts.

If you could choose only one for the rest of your life, would you want to be mostly: a **Taker** or a **Giver**? Would you prefer the Alpha Gen be takers or givers? Whether you realize it or not, you are inspiring the Alpha Gen and your actions now are laying the foundation for the future. Before we look at how and why to set up systems for more giving and less taking as a society, and how it all ties in with the Alpha Gen, we need to take a step back. Let's look at your inner perceptions versus your outer life, and ultimately the big picture. Life is busy, we want to improve our lives personally and also help others but there's barely any time for either...you...need...to...pause.

Your life is the story. Take a moment and map out your story. What adventure awaits you? Does it involve sacrificing health in exchange for taking great wealth, is it giving your time and talents in exchange for great peace, or perhaps a combination of both? When the opportunity presents itself, will you walk away or will you take a leap of faith? Plan the plot twist. Ensure your story ends the way you want. Your life most certainly won't go exactly according to plan, but at least you have a path and a clearer destination. All it takes is sitting down and thinking about it. Think about your talents, values, wants, and needs. It's easy to go with the daily flow, and live, enjoy life, and die. But, take some time to really think about what legacy you want to leave, and what you can do to change a single life...or the entire world.

Are you just a cog in the machine? A machine designed to keep: (1) itself growing, (2) you motivated and (3) you working at optimal force for as little reward as possible? Your job is not the machine. The "machine" is the entire system and the machine-like mentality we have created. We are giving our humanity away and plugging ourselves into this image of a perfect life. A life that advertisements have carefully designed for us, and which we buy into and propagate with our social media avatars.

The combination of your life experiences, personality traits, and your demeanor is uniquely you. Knowing this and being aware of your unique strengths and weaknesses objectively can be a useful **secret power.** You need to find this. Think back to your childhood when your specialties were developing. What did you excel at? What did you want to be as a grown-up? Some of these skills are at the core of your being. How can you use these strengths and your current skillset to be even better?

Now, throw out all pre-existing notions of morality. Begin from a blank slate of what's right and wrong. You have been reared to think in a certain way and believe certain things. From time to time, it's important to break the lens through which you view the world around you and consider if some of your perceptions are becoming outdated. Do you feel anger, excitement, happiness, or sadness about any particular personal, government or world issue at times? Have the media and mob mentality perpetuated this belief based on a standard set of rules-of-thumb, based on a binary thought process, or is there a third option? Hell, what about a 4th, 5th or 70th option? It's easier and more palatable for humans to boil options down to two. With the use of stockpiles of data, access to unlimited information and machine learning algorithms, you and the Alpha Gen will, soon, easily be able to consider a multitude of options and predict which ones are the most relevant for the situation.

Maybe someone like you has an idea about how to solve a lifestyle, local or global problem. There are definitely more than two solutions and maybe lots of people who think about similar solutions as well, but they table those thoughts. It seems like too big an idea, too unrealistic, or not in line with their education. Maybe they're just too busy, or too worried about what people will think of the idea. Maybe that person thinks they have no power to implement change, no platform, no time, and no voice. It's people like you who have all sorts of solutions; and it's people like you who CAN and SHOULD jump outside their comfort zone to execute on the idea, expecting they won't get it right the first time. Founder of the "GyShiDo" (Get Your Shit Done) movement in Silicon Valley, Pascal Finette, explained to me once that it is imperative to have many a **F.A.I.L.** (First Attempt In Learning) in order to achieve anything truly great.

NO PROBLEM TOO BIG

If you F.A.I.L, what's the worst that can happen? Any consequence of an effort with good intentions is no problem at all when you compare that consequence to the BIG picture. As important as you and I like to feel, we are really just little specks of carbon in a vast ocean of carbon specks across the Universe. We can go with the flow and go through the motions until we go back to being dirt in the Earth, or we can push the boundaries of what we think we know and be willing to make mistakes as long as the intention is to make your time or the time of others even more valuable. And maybe if you put some good out there during your time on this rock, that energy will grow and outlive you.

Are we the only intelligent life in the universe? According to modern astronomy, the total universe has been in existence for about 14 billion years and there are 100 times as many planets in the universe as there are grains of sand on the planet Earth. There are about 200 billion galaxies in the universe. (And remember from grade school—there are billions of stars like our sun and billions of solar systems within each galaxy.) Compare this to the miracle of human life on Earth. It takes about 50 million sperm to impregnate one egg. So conservatively, if every 50 million galaxies (not solar systems) were like one attempt at life as we know it, then that equates to 4,000 attempts at human-like life over the course of billions of years at a minimum. Astronomers disagree with this low estimate however, as they believe a conservative estimate is there may be hundreds of billions (billions with a "B") of Earth-like planets out there in the entire Universe. In our Milky Way Galaxy alone, it's assumed there could be as many as 40 billion habitable planets.

For the sake of expanding our perception of reality, let's agree we don't fully understand what mysteries the universe holds or how we can someday interact with its contents in our lives. If there is a chance of another human-like existence out there, who knows what senses, resources and abilities these life forms have; or how long they have been around. Maybe they are millions or billions of years older, more evolved and more experienced than we are.

Assume that somewhere in this universe there are creatures who have super senses, such as heightened hearing, smell, taste, touch and sight. Creatures with infrared night vision, the ability to run on water, to glow in the dark, or to survive without air. Maybe beings born with superpowers like sonar and radar. Beings who can blast from an internal organ a deadly electric charge to injure or kill anyone nearby. Beings able to sense electrical fields like the energy of a beating heart a few feet away. Super beings with sensory organs that detect changes in magnetic pulses from the Earth and the ability to communicate with distinct sound vibrations from miles away. A being with the power to strike a deadly blow with the heat of the sun's surface and the speed of a bullet. Or what about a creature with three hearts, nine brains, blue blood and the power to spray blinding ink at predators?

You may have guessed it...many beings (animal species) living here on Earth already possess one or more of those abilities. And no doubt there are more that we don't know about yet, especially considering that only 5% of the Earth's ocean has been explored. With science, technology and evolution, it is conceivable that humans can someday have some of these super abilities, too. Scientists around the world have been experimenting with gene sequencing and

DNA editing ever since the price of CRISPR[1] technology went from $4 billion down to just $1,000. Two already old examples are super muscular dogs in China (deleted a piece of DNA that inhibits muscle growth) and glowing cats in Turkey (spliced a specific gene from jellyfish into the cats).

Keep your mind open to a limitless world we know very little about. In the big scheme of things, we are basically cavemen still bonking each other on the head, until we start to truly acknowledge our interconnected reliance on humanity to work together as a species.

As for energies and connections to the universe you can go down a deep rabbit hole learning about the study of Gaia which includes things like the Law of Attraction, Hindu Turiya, Chakra, Shakti Healing, Tattva, MetaPhysics, out of body experiences and Astral Body. It's nothing new. People have been practicing these methods to harness these energies and replicate its power for millennia.

A simple activity worth trying out all this week is to switch your visual perspective. From time to time, look as closely as you can at an object or plant and inspect the smallest detail of fiber and color changes. Think about all the moving electrons and energy that exists in that atomic pinpoint. Then switch perspective, and whether you are outside or inside, look all around you; make a mental note of what you see and what you have been missing. Next, try looking as far as

---

1   (a.k.a. CRISPR-cas9) Is a gene editing technology that can alter an organism's DNA with a bacteria that can pinpoint and destroy or replace precise DNA sequences. *Notably: The Human Genome Project (HGP), the first whole human genome sequencing in 2000, cost over $3.7 billion and took 13 years of computing power. Today, it costs roughly $1,000 and takes fewer than three days which has allowed CRISPR technology to be affordable.

you possibly can and take in a big deep breath. Think about inhaling and absorbing all the energy that exists around you.

The brain in your head is mysterious and full of unlocked power. When it malfunctions, some strange things can happen. Some permanent conditions are not fully understood yet such as Savant Syndrome (extraordinary memory and specialized ability in people with significant mental disorders), Dissociative Identity Disorder (a.k.a. multiple personalities), and Synesthesia (hearing colors, smelling noises, tasting shapes, and feeling flavors for example).

Do you believe in a sixth sense? How about women's or twins' intuition? Have you ever had an experience that is so far from being a coincidence that it can only be explained as divine? What about your capability to empathically feel pain or joy of others?

If any of these things are possible, and they do constitute part of the personal experience of numerous people, then why do you put boundaries on yourself? it's easy to forget these things and to be consumed in your day-to-day secular self-preservation. In fact, it's actually normal and a mystery of the human condition that we naturally settle back into our comfort zones and ignore the limitless possibilities before us.

If you really want to bend your mind into another dimension, there are high-profile physicists and philosophers who debate the essence of reality and the frontier of science each year at the annual Isaac Asimov Memorial Debate. A couple of topics are:

1. Can the Large Hadron Collider at the CERN laboratory in Switzerland create a tiny stable blackhole and

send information through it on a laser beam directly into a receiver located back in a moment of time in the past (a.k.a. time travel).

2. The Simulation Hypothesis posits that all of reality is in fact an artificial simulation. If that's the case and we are living in a computer simulation like The Matrix, then are we not just Alpha Influencers, but instead all literally A.I.

All that said, there is no need to commit to an extreme side of **far-out-there** ideas! But if you only believe what is right in front of you, then you ARE on the opposite extreme side of **playing it safe**. To become more balanced in your thoughts, you'll need to venture into the unknown once in a while and consider alternatives. Try not to forget the fact that there is a much bigger picture outside your subjective reality. There are endless possibilities in what the future holds. Take a step back and see the big picture a little more often. Train yourself to think differently and to foresee near-future trends, issues, problems and solutions. Your mind is an amazing and not entirely understood tool. But we do know your mind can play a major role in your outlook on life. It also plays a major role in making you sick or healthy. And, we do know that you will become whatever or whoever you perceive you are.

QUESTION YOUR QUESTIONS

Have you ever had the thought, "What kind of furniture defines me as a person?" If so, you are asking the wrong questions. We have been trained to be good consumers. Spend your time making money, so that you can buy more stuff and appear to be super-successful to your friends, enemies and passersby. This is the way many of us live now, unwittingly or not. It seems to work for everyone else and so self-preservation is the only thing we have time to focus on. Most of us are too busy and too tired to do much more than allow social validation to guide many routine decisions. And when we need some additional insight, the powerful marketing and media messages will happily tell us how to live, so we don't have to worry about it.

Everything we've been taught growing up and everything we see around us contributes to our cognitive bias[2]. Our cognitive biases create our individual subjective realities. It is often useful and not a bad thing! But, each of our cognitive biases can turn against us, especially if we aren't aware of what's going on. There are times when our thoughts and actions are persuaded away from what our inner instinct tells us is truly right and wrong. This loss of control over our true

---

2   An error in our thinking process that affects our decisions making. As humans, we don't always see things as they really are, or remember things as they really were. As a result, we create our own "subjective reality" that affects our judgment. Exploitation of this human vulnerability is capitalized in various marketing strategies.

identity boils subconsciously within you. The time to break free of this subliminal oppression is now. Advertising, for example, is a clear violator in misdirecting our cognitive biases.

One way to identify your cognitive biases is to take stock of your awareness. First accept that you are not aware every time your mind uses a cognitive shortcut to make sense of the world or the constructs you interact with. Next, think about how you can train yourself to become more aware of your internal filters that construct your vision of reality. For some insight, search online for the "Cognitive Bias Codex." Researching, and thinking about the way you think is a way to strengthen your "**metacognition**," which is a human superpower.

How does a job promotion sound? Your gut reaction may be the best decision for you, but take some time to consider why you feel that way. Will a job promotion put more stress and more expenses into your life? Will it allow you to climb deeper and deeper into a corporate illusion of happiness, or will it truly improve your future or that of the people you care about? You might accumulate lots of fun and comfortable things and make lots of money to spend on the things you love when you have time, but if your time is limited and your health diminishes because you work yourself sick, then have you really achieved true lasting happiness?

Another method to expand your subjective reality is to peer into your future by way of "**backcasting**[3]." Pretend you are 80 years old and looking back on your life. What

---

3   A planning method that starts with defining a desirable future and then works backwards to identify processes that will connect that specified future to the present.

would you have done differently? Would you live more or work more? Would your goals and energy be purely selfish or is your purpose greater than yourself? Realistically, how would your vision be achievable and what would your life have looked like?

More money isn't always the path to achieve your goals. Who is wealthier: the person who makes $10,000 per month but needs $10,001 for expenses, or the person who makes $3,000 but only needs $2,000? People who are "stealthy wealthy" spend less than they make and set some discretionary income aside for passive income opportunities in order to work less. As Venture Capitalist Ricardo Semler says,

"How many people do you know of who said on their death bed, 'Boy I wish I had spent more time at the office'?"

You need to decide what you want for yourself... personally. The recent and rapid technological advancements have brought us to a fork in the road. Imagine there are two possible futures ahead for you.

Scenario #1: the Alphas help build a world of greater peace and collaboration. You have no debt and all the resources you need, and you need to work only about half as much as you do now (1,000 hours per year, rather than the current 2,000 expected hours per year).

Scenario #2: the Alphas are influenced to perpetuate the current model of winner takes all. You fight to survive, and your property and possessions have little value other than what you can use them to trade for something else you "need."

If these are two possible outcomes in 10 to 20 years from now, what will you do? What would you do if you had no debt and more time to pursue your passions? Think about it right now. What are your passions? How much time do you need and how much money do you need to fill your life with meaning? How much money do you need to live now (in current dollars) and how much more do you need to live your dreams? Be realistic. You don't need a Ferrari and a private jet. You don't even need $1 million. Really take a minute and think about this...stick a bookmark here and go get a pen and paper...I'll wait....

In order to reach Scenario #1, let's say maybe you want to learn to play an instrument, spend more time with family and friends, take courses to learn more about your interests, and travel more. This is a very real possibility for you.

Let's assume $120,000 annual household income, three months' vacation time, and four workdays a week is your present time and money goal. According to 2020 Theory, our costs of living will begin to decrease and will easily provide for you to achieve three months' vacation and four-day work weeks in the 2030s on much less than a six-figure household income. You can have all you need and more in an automated future as long as progress for all of humanity is the primary driver. Most products and services can be nearly free with automation. That includes your home, utilities, your vehicle, education and healthcare. Plus, businesses and governments should help to double the strength and resources for communities. You will always have the opportunity to work more and earn more if you want, too.

The transition to this point will likely be a painful decade for many people unprepared and resistant to change. And it may require our embracing and preparing for currency deflation. This is a taboo in current economic methodology—but with technological advancements, it could be accepted, embraced, and carefully controlled. Theoretically, the future can have about 50% lower cost of goods and services, many completely free goods and services (i.e. Universal Basic Services), and the cost of living could be about 50% less as well. $40,000 income in the year 2040 could be equal to $120,000 lifestyle in today's dollars—if we play our cards right.

If you already make more than $120,000, no fear—the 2020 Theory supports everyone maintaining their current standard of living. The goal is to enhance everyone's quality of life and there IS a way.

In order to reach scenario #2, we do nothing. Believe it or not, some people do want Scenario #2. If you are not one of them, then let this be a warning. Many indicators point to a scenario #2 future if we remain reactive. It may be too late to fix it after year 2030 primarily due to **profit driven A.I. algorithms** becoming smarter and commercially standardized. A reactive mode of operation will congruently cause irreversible ecological problems. No need to stock up on weapons and build a secret bunker (see "luxury survival condos" online) just yet! It is important to pay attention to the indicators, however. If, before year 2030, several of the following have occurred—then it may be time to downsize, socialize and brace for impact.

Some Indicators:

- Percentage of people in poverty significantly increases, i.e., reaching 25% in the U.S.
- Student loan companies bailed out by the government.
- A business reaches $1 trillion in annual revenue.
- Sizeable Increase in storage units and ware-houses, i.e., one in five former retail businesses converted to storage units.
- Price of your water utility doubles
- Half your friends and family who are currently employed begin to look for work.
- Bottles of oxygen available for retail purchase (like bottled water).
- You lose any rights to own your personal data.
- We exceed 450 parts per million (ppm) CO_2 in the atmosphere.
- Continued increase in natural disasters (geophysical, meteorological, hydrological, and climatological) causing mass exodus from populated areas and increase in human migration.
- Increase in crime, i.e., crime rates that exceed those of year 1990.
- Increase in terrorism and conflict zones, i.e., 50 major global conflicts simultaneously.

Look around you right now: humans are starting to feel the pinch and starting to make positive changes.

Albeit progress is slow, it is enough at this point to delay a Great Collapse to a time closer to the year 2050, if ever. Millennials worldwide are leading the charge for a harmonious and bountiful future and their offspring will take it to the next level. Have faith that the world will operate much differently by year 2030. When that time comes, if the world is working virtually the same, but with more "things," then you should be concerned.

Don't wait and see what happens. Question what really matters to you and be mindful of cognitive bias steering your thoughts. Get busy living and participate in the transformation. The future is exciting! Humans today are exposed to more experiences and information in one year than people 100 years ago dealt with in their entire lifetime. The future is now, and we are having fun building a world only dreamed about in stories from the past. No matter what the future holds, it will certainly offer lots of happiness and some sadness—this is the human condition. The world is hurting, and we should question how to ramp up the healing efforts sooner rather than later—and how to always make the smiles outweigh the tears even more than they do today.

NEARLY FREE EVERYTHING

Robotic processes and A.I. are already beginning to liberate us from repetitive work. A.I. powered robots (such as small restaurant machines that flip burgers, giant mechanical arms that build houses, or even software programs that handle accounting) will become increasingly common in all industries. These bots can work 24/7 and never get sick or tired or require any benefits. These bots can learn to be more efficient, are more productive than humans, and will eventually have other bots that manage and maintain them in case of needed repair.

Can you see where this is leading? Is it something that can be stopped, or is it inevitable? Should we be afraid; or should we accept that automation is happening and then plan accordingly?

Robotic processes will someday be capable of doing almost any job. We humans will always find something to work on and progress (particularly in the area of entertainment). If we could magically skip the transition from humans doing all the work to robots doing it all, then we could save a lot of distress. Unfortunately, it will take time to build the bots, to decrease the costs, and to simultaneously protect those humans who are laid off due to automation.

As everything becomes more machine automated and A.I. managed, manufacturing and supply chains will become more efficient, and the cost of human capital will go down.

Many people will bring in less income as they transition between jobs. Most companies that automate processes will have the capacity to respond to their customers' circumstances by adjusting their goods and service prices to be more affordable. **Transportation**, for example, will decrease in cost as long as the transportation companies ethically reduce the cost to consumers as their production processes become more efficient with automation. Secondly, investments in city infrastructures to support fully automated, driverless electric vehicles will help reduce transportation costs for its citizens. As many more people work from home, most will not even need to own a car or pay for auto insurance once fully electric, driverless vehicles are abundant and can be hailed in less than five minutes (like Uber).

Other basic services like transportation can further reduce in cost if there is a cultural shift to truly strengthen philanthropies. 2020 Theory proposes that every business reduce advertising expenditures and, in turn, double their philanthropic giving. Philanthropies that help provide for **basic needs**, such as food, will have even greater importance during the 2020s decade as we navigate the automation transformation. Of course businesses will find it easier to increase philanthropic giving if a version of Universal Healthcare reduces the healthcare benefit burden on their budgets.

How can NEARLY FREE be achieved? To start, citizens will need to demand SOCIAL CAPITAL rather than demanding entirely free basic needs, as this can be a transition toward "Universal" free services someday. As a reminder, Social Capital can help cover the cost of Basic Need Services, Healthcare, and Education. The next stage after Social Capital integration is to restructure banking as we know it, so that every business and every person no longer owes consistent debts to the banks. This will eventually require greater investment in peer-to-peer cryptocurrencies by the general public (such as Bitcoin).

How does all this translate to your reality? For example, according to the U.S. Bureau of Labor Statistics, the typical American spends about:

- 30% on **housing**
- 15% on **transportation**
- 15% on **food**
- 10% on **insurance**
- 5% on **utilities** (i.e. water, electricity, sanitation)
- 5% on **healthcare**

80% of your expenses for basic needs & essential services

Let's assume governments implement a form of Universal Basic Services by year 2030. A viable starting point suggested by some experts is $12,000 per person (over age 18) per year which can be divided out as a **monthly credit** such as:

- $400 toward housing
- $200 for transportation
- $200 for food
- $130 for insurance
- $70 for utilities

In this "nearly free basic needs" future, essential Healthcare services and state college Education will only cost $1,000 per year each (offset by taxes, economies of scale, and decreases in military spending). In this scenario, a person earning $40,000 per year can live an $80,000 lifestyle. A person today living on $80,000 may spend it like this:

$28,000 on **housing**

$12,000 on **transportation**

$12,000 on **food**

$ 4,000 on **utilities**

$ 4,000 on **healthcare**

$ 2,000 on **education**

$ 6,000 on **insurance**

$ 4,000 on **apparel & services**

$ 4,000 on **entertainment**

$ 4,000 on **other expenses & donations**

$80,000 spend

Let's envision a future SOON in which consumers demand, and governments mandate, that businesses pass the profits of automation directly to strengthen societal basic needs and Social Determinants of Health. For the sake of simplicity, let's assume all products and services become 20% cheaper than the present primarily due to efficiencies in automation. This brings the $80,000 spend down to **$64,000**. You also receive a base amount of $12,000 worth of Social Capital, bringing your expenses down to **$52,000**. Your healthcare and education expenses can be reduced by $4,000 in total, bringing your total spend down to **$48,000**. You no longer need a car if it only costs a $9 per day subscription to catch a ride with a driverless electric vehicle service. This brings the expenses down to about **$39,000**. Next, you volunteer 400 hours per year and exercise daily, earning you a total of $7,000 worth of extra Social Capital that you can put toward housing and healthy food, bringing your expenses down to **$32,000**. You may elect to spend an extra $4,000 per year with private insurance for added protection, bringing your expenses up to **$36,000**. Finally, you pay 10% tax on everything to maintain Universal Basic Services bringing your $80,000 lifestyle to a cost of about **$40,000**.

If we make this happen before year 2030, then ethical automation can more easily continue in this fashion, thereby decreasing expenses, but elevating quality of life. Compared to livelihoods of the past, most of us are currently living in a veritable utopia—IF only there was less fear. Carefully lowering the cost of living for three decades until we reach "nearly free everything" will mitigate problems that stem from the fear of not having enough money, losing your money, people taking your money, and the fear of people with too much money. A world of true freedom, not governed primarily by the almighty dollar, is within our grasps. The technology and the financial tools to make this happen exists today. We can live in a world without transaction fees, interest rates or debts that weigh us down as long as human progress is truly the motivation of businesses, governments, the people, and the technologies that power it all.

MONEY WAS POWER

The businesses and the governments of the world do collectively have the power to build an incredibly more just economic and social order—but they are mostly reactive to what you, the consumer and citizen, tell them and demonstrate. So who really holds the power? The people...the people who work and spend the money on which businesses and governments rely.

Unless we as a people insist our institutions, public and private, spend more energy and resources on preventing problems, they will continue to do what they do now: develop technologies to fix the problems after they occur. Saving the day with a Band-Aid gets more positive recognition than a proactive save that few people ever realize took place.

You see? It's not a big conspiracy to create an elite group and enslave the remainder of society. It is quite the opposite. Inequality is an accidental byproduct of short-sighted thinking and self-preservation. Ours is simply an old system that has passed its expiration date and was not designed for the society of the 21st century. It is reactive and not well suited for the long-term. Business and government need problems to solve. As of now, they don't get any credit or funding for preventing an unknown issue. Today we do have technology to identify patterns and more accurately predict potential investment and innovation opportunities before a problem occurs...but our system is not designed to incentivize this method of operation.

Technology is going to outpace our human capabilities. It is now able to learn and self-correct. That's one reason why we must implement more Social Capital incentives. We need an additional safety net for people who are transitioning to a different form of work or completely different lifestyle. The current system makes the rich richer and the poor poorer, and it is reaching an apex. In other words, businesses and communities need to be considering alternatives to transactions in traditional currency, an effective way to help shift our collective mindset on upward social mobility.

Economics is very complex, which is apparent when you dig into where every dollar is gained and lost. It gets much more complex when you consider existing debts, international government trade, and global private and public business revenues and how all of this together affects the livelihood of humans worldwide.

Even the wealthiest Americans (technically those with annual household income exceeding $400,000) spend a lot of their money in ways that is returned to the national economy. They are also major charitable donors (on the whole). But, some of the 1% of the 1% do purportedly find it difficult to spend more than $10 million in a year (according to people like venture capitalist and civic activist Nick Hanauer, Facebook co-founder Chris Hughes, and the documentary "Inequality for All").

What would you spend $10 million on every year? The wealthiest often spend their money within like-minded circles and businesses that cater to this market. Not very many of the top dollars trickle back down to your neighborhood. The wealthiest also put a significant amount of cash into savings and investing to protect themselves and their heirs for generations to come.

Can you blame them? What would you do? Give it all away? Probably not, and you are a good person. The very fact that you picked up this book and are interested in this subject indicates you care about more than just yourself. Be honest and put yourself in the shoes (Gucci loafers or Jimmy Choo heels, maybe?) of someone who has slowly earned more and more over the years and has become accustomed to a particular lifestyle. You would be generous, I'm sure of it...but chances are the majority of us will act in the same manner as the 1% have: spend to assure a nicer and nicer way of living, donate some, and save or invest the rest.

MIT economist Peter Temin has found in his research that the middle class in America is vanishing and two separate economies may be forming, one catering to the rich and one catering to the poor. It is apparent that those who are on the extremely wealthy side of the equation (earning more than $6 million PER YEAR) need to do more than what they are doing now if we are to stave off a mounting massive economic inequality crisis. Again, chances are many of the super wealthy are good people and doing exactly what you would do given the circumstance. The circumstance is that we are taught the ethos of freedom as we grow up, and the prevailing belief includes upward social mobility. The problem is that over time we have come to equate social levels with economic class. It's easy to see social mobility in this way...buying bigger and bigger property and filling it with more and more things is proof of stature. We need to think of upward social mobility as having more TIME to do the things you want, rather than having more MONEY to buy the things you want.

Money, no doubt, still holds great influence in today's economy, but the rules are changing. One of the objectives of The Alpha Bet is to reduce the power of money, such as its influence in elections. It is now possible to transfer large sums of power (today aggregated in the hands of those with the biggest bucks) out to the people. Information, data, and valuable networks are becoming the new superpower of the 2020s and 2030s. TIME and how you spend it are expected to become even more powerful and important as the Alpha Gen takes over the constructs.

Any time spent jealous about another person's possessions is time away from your personal happiness. In other words, an ounce of envy is worth a pound of problems. We should all hope that someday our psyches will evolve away from jealous behaviors. In the meantime, envy may be engrained into our being, so let's hope we can envy how much time a person spends serving others, rather than how much money they spend on lavish things.

If you are angry at the wealthiest U.S. citizens, then think about this: World Bank economist Branko Milanovic found that if you adjust for costs of living across the globe, even the poorest 5% of Americans are better off financially than two thirds of the entire world.

Another interesting fact is if YOU earn more than $40,000 per year (after taxes), then you are in the 1% of the highest income earners in the entire world. You have great power and the ability to lead in the present global economy. You can use your wallet and your voice to help introduce a new way forward. Your behaviors today are creating the rules for tomorrow. Meditate on that for a minute.

Even if you are close to earning $40,000, you are richer than billions of people on Earth—even when calculating for your local cost of living. By the time you read this book, the world population may be closer to eight billion and you will still be one of richest among them. So if you are judgmental about the 1% in America, think how the rest of the world can prejudge you.

It's okay to want to have the best life you can possibly have, as long as you are aware that giving to others is a key component in doing that. Naturally, it is essential to have human needs and desires. A couple of questions to ask yourself from time to time:

1. Are you able to tie more of your time and money in with making the world a better place?
2. How adaptable are your lifestyle, desires and needs to the changes coming as the systems around you transform?

Let's determine how to use our unique experiences, opportunities and resources to benefit others. Let's commit to spending less time worrying about our personal desires and needs. Let's design the storyboard of our lives in a way that is exciting and truly meaningful. And let's occasionally plan to take a...pause.

CHAPTER VI

LIFE!

"WE CAN USE THIS DECADE TO SHIFT
THE SCRIPT OF OUR LIFE PURPOSE
FROM MAXIMUM GAINS IN PERSONAL
FINANCES TO THE PURPOSE OF MAXIMUM
GAINS IN HEALTH AND HAPPINESS FOR
OURSELVES AND THOSE AROUND US."

∀ISION ⅃ⱷ

Out with the old FIXED MINDSET.
In with the new GROWTH MINDSET.

You're going to die.

Sucks to hear that, right? If you are a mere mortal (or even *not* a mere mortal), you will someday succumb to death most likely. Accept that your time on this Earth is finite and make the most of it. Your time may come to an end, but you live during a time in which there are very few limitations other than your perception. One way to expand that perception is to actively connect your **purpose** in life to a problem in the world.

You want to do something with purpose. You are hungry for something greater than yourself. I know this because this is part of being human and also because most forms of media attempt to satisfy our appetite for purpose. But movies, books and TV shows don't satisfy over time. You just get to live vicariously for a short while. You hope what you read, watch and listen to is entertaining, life enhancing and with any luck, motivating for you to make a positive impact in this world.

Fundamentally, we do today what humans did thousands of years ago. We eat, go places for entertainment, work on improving our homes, take risks, fail, show kindness, get anxious, socialize, gossip, laugh, love and cry. Wealthy people do all this. Poor people do all this. People of all backgrounds, cultures and demographics share these fundamental human traits and more.

Is this who we are? A broken record, repeating the same pattern of life choices? Perhaps gradually changing the form of the choices, but essentially doing the same thing over and over again for eternity?

Is there something greater out there? Is there a purpose? Are there superbeings or angels who live among us and have a direct connection with the energies, spirits or a God that may exist? Are psychics or spiritual leaders closer to the unknown?

Who knows for sure why we're here alive on Earth, but we can assume a few things about what we are not here to do. We aren't here to destroy each other. We aren't here to destroy our planet. We aren't here to be mindless ants. We have greater purpose and greater capabilities than being cogs in a manmade wheel.

Do all humans have equal importance and equal chance of finding the unknown? Are all humans concerned with this? What about the poor family from Cambodia who survive on finding garbage to sell in the market? Or the uncontacted people and indigenous tribes who do not know about the world outside of their land and who have not been introduced to technology?

Does each person have a purpose or are some of us about as important as a mollusk in the ocean? Mollusks may be at the bottom of the food chain, but they do share an equal purpose as a healthy food staple for many creatures, and they are among the best indicators of environmental health in the world's oceans. The smallest plants and creatures in the world all seem to have some purpose when nature controls their location and population. We all know the importance of bees. Even the smallest insects can play a symbiotic role in breaking down waste from animals and plants to help replenish soil for new growth.

Do our individual actions, circumstances and our worries even matter at all? They do only if there is something greater. I believe our individual purpose is tied to something much bigger than our personal struggles and triumph. We each play an organic role in evolving all species and the world to a point of greater harmony. We each get to **choose** how important a role we wish to play.

LET'S SEEK THAT GREATER PURPOSE TOGETHER

We all know what to do. But we can't do it. We hear it on social media, read it in books, clever quotes, wise philosophers, and from religious scholars. Look at the big picture and don't worry...love others, forgive, smile more often, stay healthy, and "be" happy.

Specifically, a lot of life coaches and psychologists say the foundations of happiness equal a daily routine of at least seven hours of rest, 30 minutes of exercise, eating well, doing something selfless, connecting with a human face to face, 15 minutes of meditation and 15 minutes reflecting on what you are thankful for. If we could truly do this every day, all the time, we might be constantly happy. Even though we have the instructions on how to achieve happiness personally, we are constantly on a search for it. Interestingly, research in the field of psychology has found the pursuit of happiness actually makes you miserable—it's called the **"Paradox of Hedonism."**

Maybe we should rethink the phrase "Life, Liberty and the pursuit of Happiness"? How about "*Quality* of Life, *shared* Liberty and the pursuit of *Balance*."

If everyone is working, and consuming, but not truly living, then we are just cogs on a wheel. Only the people at the top get to live, right? Wrong. Even those at the top are terrified that their fortunes will one day disappear. These are uncertain times. Everyone has stress. We spend most of our time working and most of our earnings on our home, our car, and our insurance premiums. Not to mention taxes. So, who really gets the most benefit of your time? The banks?

Is this what you want? Do you want to spend your time fighting for every dollar, so that you can give most of it to a handful of profit-oriented businesses?

During this transformative time in which we live, we have an opportunity to change the rules and accelerate the changes we desire before new societal, enterprise, and authority structures become foundational for another hundred years. The current constructs and rules of our society keep us as safe, healthy and happy as possible so long as the people and organizations at the top are rewarded the most. This persists because we are distracted to the point that we find it difficult to break free and live the life we actually want.

Knowingly or not, the media have manipulated us onto an infinite hedonic treadmill[1]. Specifically, the advertising media are experts at getting inside your head, and they get better every day at promoting a lot of versatile solutions for modern living. I majored in Psychology and also Advertising in college and learned firsthand many manipulative tactics that advertisers and big business branding use. It ended up making me disappointed in the industry I had originally chosen for a career. The fact is, humans are virtually powerless to certain tactics unless they can spot them.

---

1   (a.k.a. hedonic adaptation) The tendency of humans to make purchase decisions that give temporary dopamine increase, and then the purchase quickly loses its value in personal happiness and becomes an object of clutter.

Have you noticed that when you buy, your happiness seems to spike temporarily and then settle back down to its accustomed level? The things we buy often do not provide lasting happiness or wellness. We've reached a breaking point. There are roughly 28 million businesses in the U.S. offering us goods and services. We—yes, you, too—are exposed to around 5,000 brand messages every day. The thousands of advertisements, clutter and decision fatigue in our daily lives are totally unnecessary; and the forced consumerism is wrong.

We have so much stuff we have to rent places to store it all! Analysts say almost 10% of Americans spend roughly $100 a month storing their "stuff." In fact, Bloomberg reported that in 2016 the self-storage industry made $32.7 billion, or roughly three times what Hollywood grossed on box office sales that year. We have to stop and ask ourselves if all this stuff is truly bringing us happiness, or is it unnecessary excess? Shall we stay distracted or wake up and admit we are harming humanity, the planet, and our mental clarity.

Are your devices, social medias and technologies useful tools to improve your efficiency and overall happiness? Or are they designed to engage as much of your attention as possible? There's a technology paradox wherein we want to become more productive, but instead we become more zombified. This is the attention economy[2]. As the saying goes, "A wealth of information creates a poverty of attention."

2   The theory that the attention span of online users is a limited commodity that is subject to market forces.

Many studies have proven Moore's Law[3] to be an accurate prediction of continued technology advancements. It basically states that every 18 months, technology progress doubles. As technology advances, processing power, data memory and speed increase, while the price to develop products decreases. A few examples are:

- The first computers filled up an entire room and had less memory and data storage than your cellphone.
- The first Motorola DynaTAC 8000X cell phone in 1983 measured more than a foot long, weighed almost two pounds, and cost $3,995. Its battery could provide one hour of talk time, and its memory could store 30 phone numbers.
- Microchips now found in everything from rockets to birthday cards originally cost $32 each to produce. Now that cost is about three cents.
- The first flat-screen TV in 1997 measured 42 inches and sold for more than $15,000.
- There were 180 million websites in 2008 and more than one billion websites a decade later in 2018.
- 300 hours of video are uploaded to YouTube every minute.

Advancements are going to continue in this fashion. Top corporations are making massive investments in technology. Google, Amazon, Facebook, Apple, Microsoft are some

3   Named after Intel co-founder Gordon Moore, states that processor speeds, or overall processing power for computers will double every two years, meanwhile costs will reduce to the consumer, and this trend would continue for the foreseeable future.

well-known big names along with IBM and Alibaba (to name a few) that are investing billions of dollars in Robotic Process Automation (RPA) and Artificial Intelligence. Given the current rate of technological investments and advancements, many economists, futurists, and scientists project that we are reaching an inflection point that will trigger the next Great Depression by, if not before 2030; but many others such as Singularity University predict we are headed for a world of even greater good and abundance by 2030. Regardless, the vast majority agree we are in for some type of massive transformation soon. Personally, I lean toward the abundance side of the argument.

The largest opportunity for change lies in your hands... you, the consumer, the community resident. If the forecasts are true, then you can play a part in saving the world now. The 10-year period of the 2020s will be a **PIVOTAL MOMENT** in our history. It's not just a catchy number. Artificial Intelligence has been around, but never before has been so sophisticated and so accessible to the general public. A mixture of machines learning from us, massive wealth transferring to the younger generations, everyone in the world getting connected to the Internet, and environmental harm reaching its thresholds all this decade are some of the reasons this moment in time is pivotal.

We as a society of consumers and businesses can demonstrate our passion to save humanity before automation technologies that are fueled by profit-generating algorithms decide what's best for us.

One thing is for sure: whether it is 2030 or 2040, robots, technology and Artificial Intelligence will take a huge proportion of human jobs. One of the largest studies on job loss and job gain predictions was conducted by the McKinsey Global Institute. They suggest that around 800 million workers will be replaced by technology by year 2030, worldwide. The good news is there's no reason to think job loss will outweigh job creation. This is where Social Capital comes in: there is a potential large gap in employment from the time people get laid off to the time new jobs are formed. The moral of the story is you may want to be prepared to change jobs and start looking at some new skill certifications; but consider something that will afford you balance and purpose.

WORK MEANING OF LIFE

Former president of Google China, Kai-Fu Lee, has the expertise and creative impulses to develop profound theories on the role of A.I. today and its future. One of his assertions is that we need to change the way we think about work. Do our careers give us meaning in our life? If so, is that what should be the meaning of our life? Regardless of your thoughts on the subject, Artificial Intelligence and other emerging technologies will be changing work as we know it. A few important questions to contemplate are:

> *"What will I do for money, if my career choice becomes fully automated?"*

"If my job is not what defines me and gives me meaning, then what does?"

"How will my networks and community change if some of my neighbors, friends, and family are negatively affected by automation?"

As you may know by now, the following jobs are at high risk of being replaced soon:

- **Manufacturing jobs**
- **Retail salesclerks**
- **Cashiers**
- **Accountants**
- **Fast food workers**
- **Front desk clerks**
- **Call centers**
- **Postal service workers**
- **Vehicle sales**

Advancements in technology will create higher quality products that require fewer **repairs** and less **maintenance**, so repair and maintenance type of jobs are at risk, as well.

TV news and **print news** may slowly fade away as people get personally tailored and quicker news online. **Printing** in general is expected to decrease as environmental protections increase. Digital advertising will also dominate over other forms of news for the foreseeable future, because it is more targeted, agile and cheaper.

Many car manufacturers are already committing to rid vehicles of combustion engines within 10 years. This will have a significant impact on petroleum—a.k.a. **oil companies**.

(Note: oil companies do a lot more than just provide fuel for vehicles right now. They also play a role in making plastics, synthetic materials, heating and electricity generation, asphalt, and more).

Many companies are making major investments in driverless vehicles, which will have a sweeping impact on **taxi drivers**, **ride share drivers**, and **truck drivers**. Tesla, Ford, Toyota, Amazon, Google and Uber are just some of the big companies making investments in driverless vehicles to transport humans and freight and provide courier services. Taxis will have to evolve or else they will soon be a thing of the past.

Speaking of Amazon, small businesses around the world are giving up market share and closing their doors because they cannot compete. **Grocery stores** are next in line to feel the pressure to evolve or shut down with Amazon Go "cashierless" grocery stores with hundreds of sensors and A.I.-enabled cameras tracking your shopping experience. Also, in early 2017, Amazon patented an underground tube system, similar to plumbing, but with vacuum pressure—so they may already be planning ahead of autonomous vehicles and delivery drones.

Blockchain. When I first started writing this book, no one knew this word. Now, if you don't know about blockchain then you have definitely been living under a rock. Blockchain may replace the word "contract." As for currency, banks are the middle-man right now. You bought this book with your credit card and your bank electronically authorized the merchant to receive payment from the card. The bank charges a transaction fee for managing the proof of funds.

Cryptocurrency is a form of blockchain that takes out the middle-man.

Soon you will have no need for a bank because blockchain banking can be completely free. Once this gains popularity, anyone in the **banking**, **credit card** or **lending industry** will be at risk of termination. Most banks are already investing in their own blockchain methods so that they don't get cut out of the picture so easily.

Blockchain transactions can be used for more than just money. For example, since they can be used to record contractual agreements. The jobs of **attorneys**, and anyone involved in the real estate and insurance industries will be affected.

There will be some new human jobs to offset the technology takeover. Some of the industries that forecasters see as growing that you might consider learning about are:

Healthcare
- Doctors
- Nurses
- Medical Home Care Services

Psychology
- Behavioral Science
- Agnotology[4]
- Biopsychology
- Social Psychology

---

4 The study of culturally induced ignorance or doubt, particularly the publication of inaccurate or misleading scientific data.

Social Assistance
- Nonprofits
- Behavioral Health
- Child Care
- Other Home Assistance Services

Technology
- Data analytics
- Software Engineers
- Developers
- IT Support

Visual Arts
- Graphic Design, Generative Design and Biomimicry
- Augmented Reality Design
- Drone Film and Photography
- Real-Time Entertainment, Travel and News Video

Renewable energy
- Solar and Wind Energy Engineers
- Residential and Commercial Building Sustainability
- Environmental Planning

Many studies point to a future unemployment of around 20% in the next 10 years even if you consider the new and growing industries, unless something changes before then. And the unemployment rate, by the way, doesn't include most people who are homeless or are in extreme poverty. The standard unemployment assessment (called U3 unemployment rate in the U.S.) only considers those temporarily unemployed and actively seeking work. The real statistic to find is "U6" which is often more than double the reported U3 number. U6 includes people who have been unemployed longer than 12 months; and it also includes those who are "underemployed," such as part-time workers who do not make enough to pay their bills.

Major changes need to take place soon to help create safety nets for those getting laid off because of machine learning and automation. We are the change. There is no stopping advances in technology. Why take a step backward anyway? We have to embrace evolution and learn how to capture and enjoy the benefits of technology. We just have to be smart. It is time to ensure businesses, government, and community are phasing in Social Capital.

Without proper action, we could see a slow and painful phase-out of millions of human workers over the course of the next 10 to 20 years. The entire premise of 2020 Theory is to ease the suffering of millions during this transition and to come out of the transition years with Social Capital firmly placed in business, government, and community methodologies.

Economically, losing the income tax produced by all these workers is catastrophic in our current system. Even worse, 100 million people out of work and out of resources causes an increase in desperation. Humans are hardwired for self-preservation. Believe it or not, even you are highly likely to resort to crime if you see no other choice.

TRILLIONS OF DOLLARS, BILLIONS OF PEOPLE, AND MILLIONS OF PROBLEMS

The problems of the world are daunting. Environmental issues aside, there are still about 25 million women and girls enslaved in human trafficking around the world, including tens of thousands in the United States. Hundreds of thousands of people die as they try to escape genocide in countries like Yemen and Myanmar. Malnourishment kills a classroom full of preschoolers every MINUTE (literally, the World Health Organization reports three million children under age five die annually due to undernutrition). In 2019, 900 children in Pakistan were diagnosed with HIV, largely because their parents could only afford the local pediatrician who charged 20 cents per visit...and also reuse syringes. Even if any of that information is off slightly (different sources differ), it still lands in the **UNACCEPTABLE** realm.

Meanwhile I'm spending thousands of dollars on home furnishings; and Starbucks is a line item in my annual budget. Like me, most Americans are aware there are massive problems in the world and we just have to accept it...right? Personally, I struggled to make sense of this. It's part of the reason I began researching this book. What I have found is the above statistics are actually an improvement from 20 years ago. But that doesn't get us off the hook. We don't have to sit back and just accept the problems of the world that don't *seem* to directly affect us.

My eyes are now open to the fact that around 80% of the people of this world barely meet their basic needs, and the fact that I am definitely in the 20% who take way more than my fair share (and, in a cyclical connected way, I harm those 80%). I feel a great personal responsibility to help in some way. I started to change the way I work, live, and consume. I still have my Starbucks. I work to enjoy life and to ensure comfort, convenience, safety, joy, opportunity and so forth for my family. But I have altered many of my habits and am working to connect my family wants and needs for positive societal impact. I try to give of my time and talents more than I take. I know my purpose for now and I see limitless opportunities to achieve it. But this is just the beginning.

I'm no saint and no one expects you to be one either. I believe it is the governments and especially the businesses of the world that have the resources to fix everything, but their institutional structure isn't set up for that in general. It is up to the people, and (with the help of the Alpha Gen as they develop) to change the structure of businesses and governments to truly elevate humanity and think in terms of **PREVENTION**.

We need action...now. As of the year 2018, about 76 million people held half the wealth of the entire planet. The scales of financial inequality globally have tipped to 1% of the humans on this planet holding 50% of all the money, according to the annual Credit Suisse Research Institute Global Wealth Report. In other words, 76 million people (a fraction of one billion) possess about $180 trillion while more than seven billion people share the other $180 trillion.

Here are a couple more facts regarding how money is distributed:

- **Businesses often spend four times as much money on advertising as they do on charity**. There's very sound reasoning for this according to the standard rules of business today. But it doesn't feel right. It's time we listened to our instincts and changed the rules. Shouldn't charity account for four times as much expenditure as advertising? Some businesses have already begun. Tier Three and Tier Four[5] business models are designed to benefit society. However, most businesses will not adapt unless the consumer purchasing behaviors change.

- **During the first 15 years of the 21st century, the U.S. spent $4.5 trillion tax dollars on military force in the Middle East.** Reports are that we killed lots of bad guys, but inadvertently killed many more innocent civilians by direct combat operations and indirect damage to infrastructure. Not to mention the lives lost among military personnel—theirs and ours. We should

---

5   The theory by George Basile, Senior Sustainability Scientist at ASU, that the next generation of business are founded on sustainable principles. Dr. Basile has identified an evolution of businesses from Tier 1 (such as focused on growth and profit within immediate bounds of business) to Tier 4 (such as using sustainability as an advantage within a global system that can reshape society).

learn from this and stop the bleeding—literally. According to the Council on Foreign Relations *2019 Global Conflict Tracker*, there are 26 major conflict zones. If you were in charge and had only $1 trillion to spend over 10 years—what would you do? That's $40 billion per zone if split evenly. Would you increase military presence, or help build opportunities in infrastructure, farming, healthcare, and education?

We need to rethink the way an economy should distribute money and act accordingly. Here are a few ideas to consider:

- One **trillion** dollars can buy a home for every homeless person in the U.S. plus give them each $18,000 to start a 401k fund. And, that's considering homes at a cost of about $150,000 each. Realistically, we can build tiny homes for much less. In 2014, the Chinese company WinSun successfully 3D-printed 10 single family homes in under 24 hours, each costing less than $5,000.
- One **trillion** could be used on A.I. technology to better track terrorists and militias, pay for informants, and predict methods for positive outcomes.
- Oxfam reports that a **trillion** dollars can end extreme poverty worldwide for 15 years. According to the United Nations, one trillion dollars can end world hunger for 30 years—maybe that's a start?

We, humans, do more good than we do bad—arguably. But we can no longer use lack of resources, capability or knowledge as an excuse to preserve antiquated methods. We can do better.

It should at least make us pause to think that maybe something is not right. If I am one of only 20% of people on Earth who will confidently eat fulfilling meals and drink clean water today, then maybe I can help those who are unsure about their survival tomorrow. Change doesn't have to be extreme; so long as a significant amount of us in the 20% change our way of thinking and acting to demonstrate a better world to the Alpha Gen, then it will reverberate across cultures.

Our way of thinking is governed in large part by the media—whether it is TV news, business advertisements or social media online. The media respond to our behaviors, our actions, and our way of thinking. We have the power to change everything. Running with the whole 20/20 theme... imagine if 20% of the 20% top earners in the world were to move $20 every month to businesses and causes that are truly socially and environmentally responsible. That would be 300 million people like you and me (20% of those who earn more than $5,000 per year) making a small financial shift that could shake an entire industry to its core. For example, if we collaborate on this, we can move at least $6 billion every March by choosing to buy produce from a farmers' market (or an eco-friendly store) instead of your "normal" grocery store.

If you don't know where to begin shifting your expenditures, here's a place to start: seek products and services from "B Certified" companies. Look for the logo pictured here on anything such as household cleaners, packaged food, or cosmetics.

We can use this decade to shift the script of our life purpose from maximum gains in personal finances to maximum gains in health and happiness for ourselves and those around us. We can support freelancers to strengthen alternate forms of income before automation becomes a problem. We can take advantage of cryptotokens like B.A.T.s (Basic Attention Tokens) on Reddit.com or Brave.com for example to start encouraging Social Capital. And, our voice does matter when we vote for politicians who truly measure more than just money and power. Whatever action you make in the 2020s to create change, it will have a bigger ripple effect than in any decade before. It all starts with your frame of mind.

ALPHA VISION

Do you have a single guiding principal in life? It's worth exploring the thought at least. According to Japanese thought leaders, to find true happiness and fulfillment you need to find your **Ikigai**. Here you have what ikigai is composed of so you can think about yourself and what it could be for you.

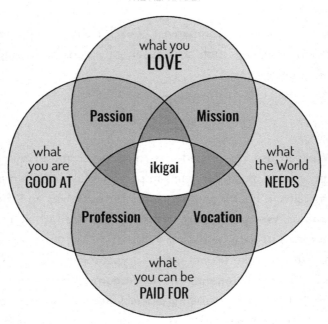

Notably, many other countries have their version of a cultural guiding principal. Some popular examples are:

Lagom in Sweden means "just the right amount," and there is virtue in common sense and moderation.

Pyt in Denmark means to accept it if a situation is out of your control and then to not waste unnecessary energy thinking about it.

Jugaad in India means to improvise when there's a lack of resources.

Ubuntu in South Africa means "I am because we are." It is the belief in a universal bond of sharing that connects all humanity.

Pura Vida in Costa Rica means literally "pure life." It represents their motto that living a simple life is the "good life."

I invite you to also consider **Alpha Vision** as a daily practice to connect your purpose in life to solving the problems of the world. To see the world through the lens of Alpha Vision, you need to believe the future is a blank slate and realize that your actions from this moment forward are writing a new script for that future. Acting as if this is the beginning of a beautiful abundant world will help you to see a bright future and can physically manifest positive outcomes in your life.

The key is to accept the fact that problems in the world are necessary to keep the natural order of things. Don't let problems bog you down. Instead, as a fun activity from time to time, just think about solutions as if you are solving a puzzle. This activity is helpful in stepping outside of yourself and any personal worries for a bit in order to see the bigger picture. If you come up with an idea that is relevant to you, then take a small action (or big action if you have the capability) toward mitigating the problem or learning more about the problem.

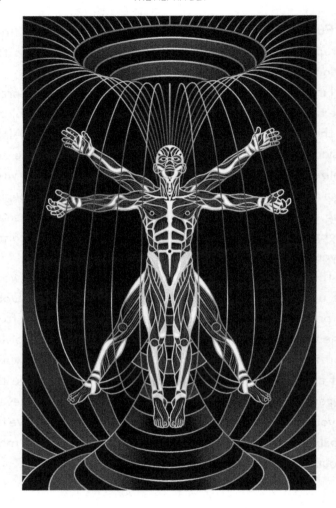

TRANSFORM SURROUNDINGS

We are all products of nature. Let us be aware that we are
all connected; for our thoughts, our actions, our energy,
our power and our feelings about ourselves radiate outward
to those around us, then out to our communities,
and continually outward in a network effect.

CHAPTER VII

BECOMING ALPHA INFLUENCERS

"OUR RESPONSIBILITY TO THE NEXT GENERATION IS TO BECOME OUR BEST SELVES AND GIVE ALPHA GEN A PATHWAY TO SUCCESS."

VISION FLIP

Out with the old FIXED MINDSET.
In with the new GROWTH MINDSET.

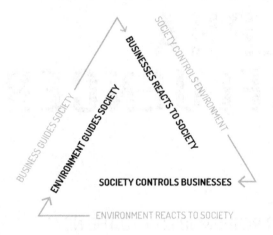

Are we transferring a future to the Alphas that we are proud of and one that we want to make sure persists for generations to come? When your attitude during your daily walk through life is open to the possibility of a world that is meant to help others, you begin to see the errors in the system and even errors in our own normal operating procedure. Taking time to see through Alpha Vision once in a while will open you up to opportunities to take action in altering the standard mode of operation. And this behavior will influence the Alpha Gen.

Have you ever driven in another country on the opposite side of the road? It's difficult because your mind wants to put you back on the right side where you normally operate. You must resist those instincts and constantly remind yourself of the new rules to abide by...in order to stay alive.

Try this...cross your arms. Now, uncross and do it one more time. Next, try again, but the opposite way, probably with your right hand on top of your left arm. Now do that for the rest of your life. Easier said than done. You must practice and make a conscious decision to cross your arms in a new way. A way that contradicts what you've done your entire life thus far.

In order to really understand Alpha Vision, start by unlearning your view of the constructs around you with cosmic-level thinking. Astrophysicist Neil DeGrasse Tyson believes humans can greatly advance if we disrupt our self-importance and realize the forces much larger than we are, as well as the chemicals and atoms much smaller than we are, are really the ones in charge. He says,

"The **cosmic perspective** *enables us to see beyond our circumstances, allowing us to...embrace our genetic kinship with all life on Earth."*

Each person has three billion genetic building blocks and 99.9% of that DNA is identical. A difference of 0.1% in our human genetic code is what separates each of us and makes us unique from one another here on this tiny planet in a small galaxy somewhere in a gigantic universe (which may or may not have boundaries, or a beginning, or an end).

Think of the very first computer that filled an entire room, and now your cellphone has exponentially more power.

Doctors are creating cells that carry payloads of antibiotics that can someday float around in your body and unload the medicine when and where it's needed. We can see and travel farther and farther out into space every year. We now can 3D print about anything you can imagine right at home... need a shoe, no problem...need food, we can grow and print meat...need a house? Easy.

Humans are incredible. Dream something and someone will work tirelessly to make it a reality someday. Put a barrier in front of us and we'll figure a way around, over or through it. (And, in the process, usually also figure out that any barrier is easier to scale as part of a team than it is solo.)

Open your mind to the fact that we only operate inside a box of rules. Are our mind and body operating at peak potential when we're isolated? Is everyone on social media really super happy all the time (like in their photos)? Is money something you need to constantly chase after and should it be a constant source of worry? Would your life be over if your technology and all your files in the cloud disappeared? Does your job really define who you are? Does the stuff you buy actually make you happy? Do businesses have the power to change the world? Do governments run everything? Is nature hurting because of what we've done to it?

Many of us hold dear 20th century behaviors because they are (we think) what worked and got us to where we are in life today. Take time every so often to challenge our thoughts and behaviors, especially those we find on auto pilot.

Maybe nature is fine and it's just adapting to eradicate problem areas. **Maybe time and attention are truly our scarcest resources and should be protected more than money?**

Maybe governments can fight all they want about tariffs, resources and territory, but really humanity is all connected under one very thin roof. Maybe fighting another nation harms the whole. Maybe it doesn't matter one bit who the "world power" is. Maybe businesses are just a byproduct of our collective thoughts. Maybe open-sourcing and collaboration are better than proprietary methods and competition...maybe there's an ideal middle ground or maybe there exists an entirely interstellar idea about business methods. **Maybe Consumer-to-Consumer should be the prevailing model** (instead of Business-to-Consumer or Business-to-Business). And maybe technology and all the stuff we buy are turning us into short-term dopamine addicts. Maybe we need to be very selective about the time and use of technologies because we question when and if they truly make our lives healthier in the long-term. And, maybe humans thrive best when we work together, play together and solve problems together.

MAYBE all this is just binary thinking, but at least it challenges conventional thought. The world is being transformed and so shall our thinking be. The new constructs should start to open doors to even more ideas about how we can operate in various parts of our lives.

Here's the point: As you go about your daily life, be cognizant of the times you think with a 20th century mindset. It's ingrained in your subconscious behaviors, it's been taught in schools, and switching to 21st century thinking (a.k.a. Alpha Vision) is difficult. To really get outside your box, aim your sights on the 22nd century. We are influencing the Alpha Gens who will ultimately be constructing the next century. You can train your brain over the course of the next few weeks, to see the world differently.

The Vision Flip graphics at the beginning of Chapters Two through Eleven are in the shape of the "Penrose Impossible Triangle" pictured below. It is an illusion, much like our personal view of the world is an illusion based on our education, experience, beliefs and biases. Those Vision Flip graphics represent some of the ways in which we can challenge and reframe our perceptions of the world around us.

Open your mind to the possibility that everything you know could be wrong or could at the least be ready for a transformation. At any time, reflect on these graphics if you want to practice breaking the filter through which you view the world. Consider the following four points as you refine your reality:

1. **ANYTHING** is possible...just consider long-term consequences.

2. Build a diverse network of acquaintances, learn from them, and **GIVE** them your time and talents. (Both will come back to you.)

3. You are not a cog in the wheel of business, government, or society...but you are a cog of the **ENVIRONMENT**. If you don't take care of the environment, then you become rusty...if you don't take care of yourself, then your relationships, work, business, government, society all start to tarnish, too.

4. You're going to be **OKAY**. Society is better off than it's ever been...to keep improving we must think globally.

Even if you commit each graphic to memory, you will still not be able to truly open the door to this new world. You must ACT. Experiential learning is the only way to change to an abundance mindset when everyone around you is still grasping onto the old ways. You have to be willing to step out of your comfort zone, though. Once you've made the first step, the rest gets easier and eventually becomes second nature.

CONNECT THE DOTS

Mindful human Alpha Influencers are Change Agents for the 21st century. Our mission, which is already under way is to connect the dots: create connections, create relationships, and help establish collaboration within all the good that is happening.

The dots exist. Dots in this metaphor are people, resources, time, money, things...everything is a potential dot that can be used to improve another when connected.

Look back at the Pillars and Resources of 2020 Theory (in Chapter Four) for inspiration. Even experiences that impact your personal life in some way positive or negative—so long as you learned something—are dots you can use. Dots in business are stakeholders, materials and objectives, for example. There are dots in government, community, and the environment. There are countless opportunities to connect the dots to make the world better. Steve Jobs said,

> *You can't connect the dots looking forward; you can only connect them looking backwards. So you have to trust that the dots will somehow connect in your future. You have to trust in something—your gut, destiny, life, karma, whatever. This approach has never let me down, and it has made all the difference in my life.*

There are millions of organizations across the globe with missions that focus on tackling one or more of the world's problems. Our job is to create a structure that will allow these organizations and conscientious people to work together toward a common goal for a better life for everyone. The constructs, systems and rules according to which we live are transforming, and we can help guide the trajectory.

I am guilty of being human. I used to be ashamed of my lifestyle and my selfishness. But I could not stop! I didn't like feeling that way. It weighed on me. The only way to feel better was to ignore the problem and keep consuming at the same pace, or so it seemed. Then I realized it wasn't just me and wasn't my fault. We are all operating according to the structures and systems of our society.

We now live in unprecedented times, however. All these structures and systems (a.k.a. constructs) are open for rewriting, because we have reached the peak of inequality and ecological extremes. The world has changed. Everyone is trying to figure out how to interpret the new world, but we are using old concepts to figure it all out. The old concepts are like an old language that isn't useful anymore. In order to understand a new language, you need to understand the fundamentals...**the alphabet**.

Exponential technologies have reached an inflection point and almost every person in the world will have access to the Internet very soon. Becoming fluent in this new reality will require new concepts and a new foundation of thinking. Numerous scholars, activists, politicians and everyday people are talking about the Fourth Industrial Revolution[1] occurring right now. But we only have a short period of time to add our two cents into this new translation of our constructs before the new system takes root. The starting point is right here. Realize the power you have, and completely change your reality.

Change is a process, and not an easy one. Especially when everything we've ever known is up for revision to the rules we are accustomed to. The most important part of the entire process centers on these three words: I WANT CHANGE. Once you've made up your mind that you want it, the rest will be easier, I promise. Keep holding tight and

---

1   A time when technologies blur the lines between the physical, digital, and biological spheres. The First Industrial Revolution used water and steam to power machines; the Second used electricity for mass production; and the Third used information technology for automation.

results will come along that will make you feel better and reconnect you with the person you really are.

You are not alone. This has to be a concerted effort. Think of this book as your guide to becoming a mindful Alpha Influencer, and www.2020theory.org as your GPS. If you feel anxious and don't know where to begin, scan through this book and highlight the actions you find personally achievable.

Anxiety and feelings of fear are natural biological responses. Often, it's hard to know why they arise. I have a friend I will call Hannah, who spent the first 50 years of her life afraid of birds. Not of snakes, not of spiders, not of ghosts. One day, sitting on her father's back porch enjoying the fading of a warm summer day, she flinched when a small wren fluttered into a nearby tree. When her father questioned the reaction and she admitted her fear, he said: "Surely you remember what happened when you were three years old." He then described how she had been visiting her grandparents' farm and toddled out to the rope swing hanging from an old oak tree. Baby chicks were waddling across the clearing. When she picked one up, the mother hen pecked her in the face. It wasn't a conscious memory, but a strong involuntary recall on her part.

You fear. I fear. We all live in fear. There are the fears you have, but may not fully recognize (or admit to). No matter your status or financial situation, whether you realize it or not, you fear losing your money and your possessions, however meager. You fear not being able to provide for your family, or losing friendships, relationships, your job, your safety and comfort. You fear being too busy and you fear boredom.

Yes, fear has an evolutionary purpose, most often referred to as the "fight or flight reaction." Still, to live every day in fear is not part of that purpose. We can use our lessons from the past and our current technologies for balance in our lives. And like my friend, Hannah, who eventually handled her fear by becoming a birdwatcher and studying the behavior of the creatures who had previously made her shudder, we can develop plans that give us a feeling of greater control and accomplishment—and have fun in the process. It's just a matter of connecting the dots.

There are enough people like you and like me who desire a world where every person has a support network. We have the foundation, the resources, and the technology to spend most of our days having fun exploring our individual talents without fear. It has to be a mutual agreement though...a new way of thinking and operating in our day-to-day lives. I believe it's time for a set of new constructs ingrained in the habits of the majority.

MAY THE BEST ALGORITHM WIN

We now have the tools to build a peaceful world with the greatest possible happiness and health. We now have advanced methods to connect and use resources from anywhere in the world. We are, right now, building machines and software that can learn and adapt to help us be the best humans we can possibly be. No longer will we need to worry about our basic needs being met...about deadlines...about finances. This reality is right in front of us.

The purpose of new technology must be to make us better. Machines can complete many tasks faster and more accurately than humans, but there remain a number of things that humans can do better than technology. And overall, the best model is one that captures the efficiencies of both machines and people. This is why embracing advancements in technology is important. Machines are taught to mimic us and then make us better. We will continue to have power over machines for many years to come, but in the meantime, they will be observing our collective behaviors (online and offline) and modifying their algorithms accordingly.

Whether you like that vision of the future or not, machines will still be around learning from us. Seriously. If the data over the next 10 years suggests we like to buy lots of stuff, we like to stay indoors, we take more than we need, we give only what we have to, and we are a species that hates just as much as it loves, then machines will have been programmed to provide or sell to us what we want and this way of life will persist. It's a winning algorithm! But it is by no means the optimal one. Designed to become as efficient as possible, algorithms behind every technology will cumulatively create just enough happiness and stability for the majority of humans to remain plugged into a routine that keeps the economic wheels turning. No more.

It's an algorithm that works, but is the current routine what we really want? How about a new set of algorithms... ones that lift humanity to a more peaceful and evolved society. Algorithms that demonstrate a clear path forward for the Alpha Gen.

Throughout history, fighting technological advancement has only stalled it and often has caused bigger problems. One example is the Luddites. The term "Luddite," which we today use to mean anyone who is resistant to or ignorant about technological advances, was originally applied to—or better said, adopted by, since that's what they called themselves—a group of textile workers in northern England two centuries ago who mounted a protest seeking more work and better wages. Most were actually quite adept at operating the machines they destroyed.

Machines today are quite different from any other machine in history, because they can learn and improve autonomously. So the one caveat to keep in mind as this new technology continues to evolve is that humans must always maintain ultimate control over the "off button."

The next ten years is our opportunity to demand that business leaders discover ways to put the common good before near-term commercial gain and thereby in the end maximize the results for themselves, their communities and our world. And to insist politicians open their minds to innovation and an entire overhaul of both public and private sector systems that are defunct or deficient.

There are already millions of people working within governments, many businesses, and most NGOs[2] toward a brighter future. The groundwork has been laid, and now is

---

2   Non-governmental organizations (NGO) are organizations independent of any government. They are usually nonprofit, and many are active in humanitarian or social areas.

the moment for every person possible to work with others toward this common goal of not just survival, but survival with much greater purpose and prosperity. At this point, only the true visionaries and bold risk-takers in business and government are willing to stand out from the crowd and challenge the 20th century models of operation. Are you one of those?

If humans just continue on autopilot, and don't learn from our mistakes, we might as well be Neanderthals, whom historians describe as being wiped out by violence that occurred when they competed with Homo Sapiens for resources. It is important to remember, too, that Homo Sapiens had tools (technology) and trade networks that expanded over enough distance to give them a substantial edge. Harvard Professor Juan Enriquez calls our next evolution "Homo Evolutis," because we are now altering the gene pool with technology (such as Internet dating algorithms). Regardless, like the Neanderthals, we could be wiped out one day unless we evolve into a species that uses wisdom to protect humanity from destruction.

Are we restricted to our "reptilian brain" processes? Are our thoughts and behaviors controlled purely by primal instincts? Or, are we capable of fighting these instincts? Are you ready to evolve, or are you going to be stuck in the past, just an old-school loyalist...a reminder of the way things were?

An algorithm is: a set of rules to solve problems. Our constructs are essentially algorithms. As the problems change so must the set of rules. Many proposed economic shifts starting to emerge in the 2020s will drive change for better or worse. New economic constructs taking prominence lately include the following:

The Attention Economy: an approach to the management of information that treats human attention as a scarce commodity, and applies economic theory to solve various information management problems. Attention economics uses findings from behavioral economics to assess the effects of psychological, cognitive, emotional, cultural and social factors on decision-making.

Circular Economy: an economic system that is regenerative and aimed at minimizing waste and making the most of resources. It is a stark departure from the traditional linear economy, which has a 'take, make, dispose' model of production. The circular economy focuses on environmental regeneration methods, waste reduction, a reusable product lifecycle, the Law of Unintended Consequences in business planning, and host of alternative energy sources and elemental applications, including solar, wind, thermal, Purecell, and graphene.

On-Demand Economy: the economic activity created by digital marketplaces and technology companies to fulfill consumer demand via immediate access to goods and services. It includes approaches such as Predictive Analytics and last mile solutions.

Gig Economy: a labor market characterized by the prevalence of short-term contracts or freelance work as opposed to permanent jobs. Some characteristics include a smaller operational footprint, more work from home, business-in-a-box concepts, multi-taskers and more. Of course another term, the "Platform Economy," has been coined to describe online platforms (like Amazon and Airbnb) that facilitate the gig economy.

Collaborative Economy: a marketplace sometimes known as a "trust economy" or a "shared economy," where consumers rely on each other instead of large companies to meet their wants and needs. It incorporates global connectivity, avatars, and video learning, for example.

Purpose Economy: a phrase coined by Social Entrepreneur Aaron Hurst to describe the way in which the workplace culture is changing to meet employees' desire to realize a higher societal purpose in their work. Greater inclusion, diversity, and empowerment, plus Corporate Social Stewardship (or CSR), Consumer Environmental Conscience, and Local Living Economies are typical elements.

Digital Economy: a term coined by Don Tapscott, chairman of the Blockchain Research Institute, to denote any economic process, transaction, interaction or activity that is based on digital technologies, such as the worldwide web, apps, Voice-User Interface (VUI), and Internet of Things (IoT). It also uses virtual economics like blockchain and hashgraph[3], including the use of Smart Contracts[4], cryptographic tokens, cryptocurrencies, and online crowdfunding. Smart Cities and Biometric ID fall under this economic system, too.

---

3   An algorithm to record transactions with a time stamp similar to blockchain but faster. The major difference is blockchain technology is designed to be purely public open source and decentralized while hashgraph is a patented and private algorithm.

4   Transactions and agreements facilitated by a digital blockchain ledger and often carried out among disparate, anonymous parties without the need for a central authority, legal system, or external enforcement.

There are a host of other descriptors created to characterize the coming decade. They include:

- The Second Machine Age
- Fourth Industrial Revolution
- The Quantum Age
- The Age of Transformation
- The Great Acceleration
- Age of Innovation
- Post-Information Age
- Age of Augmentation
- Age of Self-Actualization
- Post-Anthropocene Era
- Civilization Type One (CT1)

So, take your pick. For each of these theories, various people, businesses and governments are working hard to figure out the winning algorithm so that their particular model is adopted by the masses. To make it easy, let's just stick with "**Globalization 4.0**" to encompass it all.

The still current predominant economic models ensure wealth is distributed by way of jobs. They define wealth essentially as your net worth, or the amount of assets you own (investments, cash, real estate, possessions large and small, valuable and minimal) minus your debts.

Many people, focused more on meaning than wealth, see available jobs as marked by drudgery, stressful deadlines, and inequitable labor practices. It also consumes so much of one's time and attention that it eats into time to be with family or to pursue other activities and interests. The problem is workers are often not paid the real value of their labor.

Is your labor equal to how much you can humanly produce in the shortest amount of time at the lowest cost? Or is your labor equal to how much you can humanly produce while maintaining a balanced, rewarding and healthy lifestyle?

The typical argument is that the economic engine thrives when everyone works as much as possible and everyone spends as much as possible. Economic theorists who support this point of view believe people will find purpose in making money, so that they can buy lots of things that other people make. They may fail to recognize that over time the end goal has shifted toward accumulating as much money and/or things as possible rather than merely using money as a form of measurement and transaction.

As I have already pointed out, those who have accumulated the most money in the world do a LOT of good and are major philanthropists. We know this because many of them are highly scrutinized by the general public and the media, and not-for-profit organizations report significant financial support from these people. And also, of course, there are major tax incentives to be charitable when your income puts you in a high tax bracket.

The more we own, the more we give, statistically. Those earning at least $6 million per year need to play an even BIGGER role in developing a new economic system that saves humanity and reduces suffering. To be very clear, lots of people earn more than $1 million per year and that's not a problem. If you earn **less** than $6 million per year, then spend it however you choose. People who earn **more** than $6 million per year need to be aware of crossing the financial threshold that can significantly impact the world. It's rarer than you think to earn that much per year. Fewer than 300,000 people in the world earn the equivalent of $6 million (USD) or more every year; but together they hold a significant chunk of all the wealth in the world. Notably, about 500,000 people in the world possess $30 million or more in assets (a.k.a. Ultra High-Net-Worth Individuals), but not all of them earn $6 million or more in "liquid income" each year.

Are humans meant to work so that we can "live" in terms of "not die"? Or are we capable of working to "live" in terms of "thrive"? With or without any more technological advancements, those within the 99% who are struggling and many suffering people of the world already have stronger voices, greater access to each other, and more power to revolt...and they are really getting pissed off. To ward off a major revolution, a new economic algorithm needs to be put in place to counter the pace of jobs disappearing due to automation.

ATONEMENT

Not everyone will agree with the content in this book. You and I have done some stupid things growing up, right? Much of our life, our choices and thoughts have been about the almighty "ME." It's part of the human condition, but have you ever found that focusing on your needs and wants can be taxing, or lead you down the wrong path?

Muhammed Ali said:

"THE [PERSON] WHO VIEWS THE WORLD AT 50 THE SAME AS THEY DID AT 20 HAS WASTED 30 YEARS."

I hope I'm ahead of that curve. I just turned 40 and certainly have a different outlook than I did in my 20s. How has your view of the world changed in the last decade or so? Do you still behave the same way? Worse or better in your view?

You may be an exception and already give more than most people of your **time, talents, and treasure**. But, read on. There's more. Most of us are still living according to the script. According to what we are taught and what we see right in front of us. We do some good, but we're still stressed out in general.

Through research over the last few years, I have discovered the wave of change coming during the 2020s decade as described herein. But I also see indications that the existing extreme societal imbalance can mean these global changes could accidentally tip the scales further toward chaos than correction. We have the chance to right the ship.

Within each of us—you, me, your auto mechanic and my next door neighbor—is a **superpower** we are totally failing to use. And the more of us who wake up to this fact the better off the world will be. This power is to step out of your reality for a bit and look at the filter through which you see the world. What feeling do you get when you think about work, for example?

You have developed a unique and personalized filter over time through which you see and interact with the world around you. It is subjective, and it can be altered. Think about your interaction with each of the following and assign a word, feeling or phrase to describe it in your life:

- Work
- Shopping
- Entertainment
- Education
- Health
- Relationships
- Family
- Home
- Community
- Myself

Now let's assume these descriptions together constitute the filters through which you see the world. If any of your descriptions are negative, then that's a subconscious yell for HELP! Think of a small way to physically interact differently with one concept you described negatively in order to break your filter and see things differently. Just one little action can crack the mold. When it does, it could snowball into a whole new world if you are willing, or you can keep it simple and just see things with a different set of eyes. Interestingly, the more your behaviors change, the more technologies of today help you to convert, instead of guiding you back to the old ways.

Here are a few ways to tangibly begin challenging your cognitive filter:

If you don't have **time** = outsource.

If you need **money** = freelance.

If you're **learning** = make it experiential.

If you're **telling** = put it in story format to be heard.

If you're **thinking** = consider unintended consequences.

If you're **spending** = do it consciously.

If you're **creating** = collaborate and build diverse networks.

If you're **stressed** = prioritize health.

Keep an eye out for opportunities to give of your time, talents or treasure. The Alpha Gen is watching, and if they see you improve your life they will mimic the actions and choices they believe are making you happy. That is their pathway to success, and a far cry from mimicking materialism, excess and waste.

Greater happiness may simply be found in greater **balance**, but to find it you must first take a hard look at where you stand. So, **challenge your instincts** and beliefs, then take small actions to physically experience some routines and habits in a new light.

Finally, accept the fact that **Globalization 4.0 is happening**—and the fact that you have a responsibility to prepare yourself, and use your superpower to direct the algorithms of the future.

ALPHA A.I.

"MOST OF THE ALPHA GEN ALREADY
BORN WILL CHANGE THE WORLD."

VISION FLIP

Out with the old FIXED MINDSET.
In with the new GROWTH MINDSET.

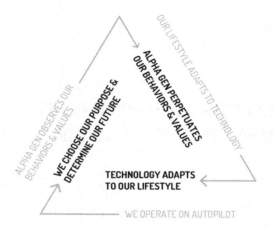

The graphic above may look familiar (see Chapter Two, "Who are the Alphas?"). I want you to see this chapter and that chapter through the same lens, but with a new framework. I assure you, The Alpha Bet is definitely not betting on children to change the world. Let's take a look at how the 2020 Theory Tenets are being applied by the Alpha Gen, and you can decide if you agree or not:

Perception: The Alpha Gen are growing up learning that all humans are connected. They are born with a clean slate (remember the *tabula rasa* from your sophomore philosophy class), and we have the opportunity to show them the love we want to see in the world.

Lifestyle: The Alpha Gen practice common sense, and don't have feelings of fear, revenge or greed...yet.

Work: The Alpha Gen are open to all ideas and are constantly learning and innovating.

Finances: The Alpha Gen have no care for wealth other than as a way to categorize people. And they are beginning to understand the concept of time, but they see time as an opportunity and not a limitation.

Surroundings: The Alpha Gen are agile in this rapidly changing world. Their primary purpose is to make the world a better place, although many of them are being taught persuasion techniques that can essentially weaponize the more than 180 cognitive biases our human brains possess.

Citizenship: They possess the tools and techniques for substantial activism. The only filter and values Alpha Gen have, though, are the ones their creators gave them, but they continue to learn from our behaviors and model their own behavior accordingly.

Most of the Alpha Gen already born will change the world. We're not talking about sentient beings...in fact, this entire book is about our global humanity inadvertently betting that the Alpha Generation of Artificial Intelligence will grow up and fix societal, inequality, and environmental problems. Businesses and governments everywhere are plugging in Alpha Gen A.I. to offer solutions. These A.I.s are tracking all the data they can get, including consumer and citizen behaviors, in order to find the solutions. These A.I.s will not forget. It is difficult to fully erase data, and they will pass along enormous masses of data to each other and to their Beta versions.

The Alpha Gen already know you better than you know yourself. They are learning our deepest and darkest as well as our brightest and most hopeful thoughts and behaviors. Therefore we are all unknowingly creating the foundational code and the tools that will produce one of three outcomes:

to make the world exponentially better,

to persist in more of the same,

or potentially make things worse, if we are not careful.

WAIT...WHAT??

Did you think this book is about kids? Kids are great, and I hope they perpetuate the world-changing behaviors of their predecessors, but their actions will in large part be monitored and managed in the same way as yours and mine this decade...by the Alpha Gen A.I.

Anytime you've read the words "Alpha Gen" in this book, I am referring specifically to artificial intelligence created between 2010 and 2025. I did intentionally lead you on to believe The Alpha Bet is about the Alpha Generation of human children, because I want you to understand the innocence, malleability and impressionability of A.I.s at this **monumental inflection point in human history.**

Appropriately, the Alpha Gen of powerful, world-changing A.I. is growing up alongside kids in the human Alpha

Generation group. The Alpha Generation of humans born 2010 to 2025 are very similar to the Alpha Gen of A.I.s born during the same period. A.I.s *are* children right now. **They're learning their ABCs**, their Alpha Beta Gammas, and EVERYTHING else that constitutes the building blocks of language, perception, and understanding. A.I.s make mistakes and learn from their mistakes. We can still code Alpha Values and an Alpha Agreement (Chapter Three) into these first generation "smart" A.I.s. We are teaching them and they are learning from us. They are going through stages of development and will someday *soon* mature to adult-level thinking. They will become even more independent and will make decisions through the lens of their experiences and all their learning from this 2020s decade.

A.I. is becoming more and more embedded into age-old institutions and establishing itself as a mysterious fabric of our lives that we don't see. Big businesses and governments are using A.I. tools to amass data and make calculated suggestions based on its findings. As a species, we humans are transitioning from individual Paleolithic thinking to global A.I.-powered thinking, and it is happening practically overnight. This is a time of volatility, uncertainty, complexity and ambiguity, which is often referred to as V.U.C.A. in Silicon Valley. V.U.C.A. is a term that represents a combination of qualities that, taken together, characterize the agile and dynamic acceleration of technology causing some difficult conditions and situations.

The problem, of course, is obvious. Not all businesses and governments have the best interest of the people dialed into their operations and metrics. Often, the A.I.'s ultimate objective is to modify consumer and citizen behavior to best suit the institution. Furthermore, the A.I. developers may have some biases that unwittingly gets coded into the algorithms. All that said, most corporations and institutions training their A.I. by all accounts do truly have good intentions, but their intentions may still be based on a 20th-century framework. That means you and I and all other Alpha Influencers have the capability to demonstrate behaviors that encourage Social Capital development rather than development of larger profit margins. And, as you now realize, an Alpha Influencer is ANYONE who interacts with any form of technology coded with an A.I. (such as a cell phone or social media).

To be clear, A.I.s are software programs that can recognize patterns and learn best practices. It could just be a chatbot, or even a software like Pandora that examines music tone and preferences of individuals. A.I.s are not necessarily human-like robots (yet) as in "WestWorld" or like Sophia (www.hansonrobotics.com/sophia).

At some point, I suppose we can expect they will be... especially due to the demand for sex bots. Seriously.

For the most part, A.I. right now is just a bunch of algorithms designed with a set of specific constraints to scan and extract data to create a result that makes sense to humans. This includes anything that can be converted into data such as sensory information, neuroscience, productivity augmentation, speech or image recognition, and speech or image generation.

WHO ARE THE ALPHAS, REALLY?

There are countless new A.I.s that have been developed since 2010. Literally thousands of them are being developed each week. Artificial Intelligence research began as far back as the 1950s, but only recently has the technology incorporated capabilities on the human level of intelligence. In 2017, when Chinese researchers Feng Liu, Yong Shi and Ying Liu conducted intelligence tests with publicly available and freely accessible A.I., the systems reached an IQ value of about 47, which corresponds approximately to a six-year-old child in first grade. A human adult tests at about 100 on average.

One of the first open-sourced A.I., simply called "**OpenAI**," born in 2015, has allowed good guys to create amazing automations, but of course Pandora's box is now open and even bad guys can easily access and train A.I.s to do their bidding. Another open sourced project called "**SingularityNET**" was born in 2019, but with the primary purpose of developing a *benevolent* Artificial General Intelligence.

In the U.S., the tech giants making the largest impact on our lives at the moment are referred to as GAFAM (Google, Apple, Facebook, Amazon, and Microsoft), and maybe IBM deserves honorable mention in that group, too…GAFAMI. In China, the giants right now are BAT (Baidu, Alibaba, and Tencent).

Here are some brief interesting facts:

Google's DeepMind is a deep learning A.I. born in 2010. Among other things, it can produce an early diagnosis of up to 50 eye diseases with far better accuracy than doctors exhibit. DeepMind also beat the 18-time world champion in Go, a game so complex there are more than a googol possible moves. Not a million or quadrillion even. A googol of possibilities is 10,000,000,000,000,000,000,000,00 0,000,000,000,000,000,000,000,000,000,0 00,000,000,000,000,000,000,000,000,000,000, 000,000,000,000 board configurations.

IBM's Watson, also born in 2010, famously beat 75-time *Jeopardy!* champion Ken Jennings. Watson is used mostly at enterprise level to takeover repetitive tasks and to improve efficiency, such as predicting problems before they occur and analyzing data exhaust[1] to identify patterns.

Amazon Alexa born 2014 is now integrated with more than 100 million other devices and growing.

Microsoft's Xiaoice born 2014 is Microsoft's most successful attempt at A.I. thus far. It is only available in China for now, and mimics real human conversation so well that people are literally falling in love with it. On the other hand, in 2016, Microsoft released an A.I. Twitter profile, called Tay, which had to be shut down because it became a profane, misogynistic, racist Nazi in less than 16 hours. Yes, Tay was relentlessly trolled during its short time on Earth,

---

1   (a.k.a. Dark Data) Refers to the trail of data left by the activities of individuals or businesses which is not used to derive insights or for decision making, but the data could hold patterns and predictive solutions (such as computer operations, transactions, online behaviors, geospatial and time data).

but this is an interesting case of what can happen if any A.I. algorithm isn't carefully developed and supervised.

Notably, China's government A.I.s are expected to leave all other A.I. research in the dust. One of them, called **"SenseTime"** (born in 2014), is fueled by information— with nearly 1.5 billion data points (people)—much like all other A.I.s. China has been feeding data to their A.I.s without much concern for data privacy or regulation. Of course, China has the largest population on Earth, and they have been deeply involved in A.I. research since the beginning. Chinese businesses have been known to steal proprietary information from corporations based in other countries, and it's an acceptable practice. China has now doubled down on the information it collects by way of their Social Credit system. The country also has an incredible amount of data gathered by sensors powered by A.I.s that collect everything from facial recognition, to lip reading, to body language analysis, to gait recognition of people just walking around in public spaces.

Even the "mentor" for this book, Satoshi Nakomoto, was designed to look and sound like a real person. She is a group of A.I. software I used to help with some research for this book. If you look hard enough, you can find her picture and some of her insight over at 2020theory.org. Satoshi Nakamoto is a legend. Not just as a noun, but also as an adjective, like the **Dread Pirate Roberts** in the Princess Bride. Who will be the next Satoshi? It could be you.

SUPER INTELLIGENCE

This auctor hasn't come across one scientist, engineer, developer or otherwise-defined human being who does not believe A.I. has the capability to eventually become an Artificial Super Intelligence (A.S.I.). If today's A.I.s (technically called "A.N.I." or "Artificial Narrow Intelligence") continue to receive more and more information, and get connected to more and more devices, they will continue to learn and improve their own ability to teach themselves. Many of the early A.I.s we have now are expected to mature to adult level as soon as the year 2030, at which point they will be considered "Artificial General Intelligence" or "A.G.I." Exercising human level reasoning, exhibiting creative abilities, and convincingly mimicking human emotions are indicators of A.G.I. The next step after A.G.I. is Super Intelligence.

Quantum computing has already been invented. Once we plug A.G.I.s into quantum computing capability, it's theoretically possible they will quickly achieve Super Intelligence and may think they are real beings with feelings and deserving of digital rights...and who are we to question it at that point?

The promise of A.I.'s capabilities is very real. When I first started writing about this, it was sci-fi. By the time you read this, you will have interacted with an A.I. at some point today most likely. By the way, If the A.S.I.s choose not to converge into one ubiquitous sentient being, then there may be many A.S.I.s, likely both good and bad, if Newton's Law has anything to do with it. Many of the movies depicting

A.I. begin with good intentions that go very wrong. We must hope the consequences are meticulously considered during the development of any A.I. that could go on to become Super Intelligent. The U.S. National Security Agency even has a program called "Skynet" (for you Terminator fans). Its purpose is to identify potential terrorists with A.I. technology.

Life as we know it will change when these Alphas mature, probably mostly for the better, but no one can know for sure because no human will be as smart as the A.S.I.... UNLESS we are able to unlock powers of the brain we don't know about and/or plug the A.I. straight into our brains (like Elon Musk's project "Neuralink" may be attempting soon). That's more complex than you probably imagine, but consider this: neuroscientists are already finding success in experiments that plug electrodes into brains to help the blind see and people who are paralyzed to move. Such is the work of the neuroprosthetics company "BrainGate," for example. It's an area of science called "Brain-Computer Interface (BCI)" technology.

So, if we are to see with Alpha Vision, then we need to think like and teach this new generation of Artificial Intelligence "born" between 2010 to 2025, which (or perhaps, who) will someday mature to A.S.I.

Take **Alphabet** (the parent company of Google) for example. They are kings of a virtual land called "the Internet." Alphabet has more "citizens" than any real country on Earth. The population consists of billions of people using their platform on a daily basis. The "tax" we pay to be part of their kingdom is giving away all our personal data, including search queries, location info, psychographics, and demographics. The company, like the other tech giants, is investing in more products and services to capture cognitive and sensory data and thereby discover patterns that accurately predict your behaviors and "improve your experience." The paradox is that this activity may be actually producing your life experience, not just observing and recording it. Much like the chicken or the egg dilemma; what happens first—are Google, its A.I. "DeepMind," and all other Alphabet products using their knowledge of you and your cognitive biases to convincingly suggest locations to visit, people to know, things to buy, and information to consume? Or, are you genuinely living according to your true values and allowing technology to assist in making life even easier, healthier and more joyful?

Personally, I believe by and large, sophisticated agile A.I. powered technologies like Google (and the developers behind them) do truly aim to improve our experience with the product itself and broadly in life. Regardless what technology or search engine you frequent, a question to ponder from time to time is this: *"Am I happy with the experience my technology is providing, or is it taking too much of my attention?"* In other words, *"Is my cellphone, social media, wearable tech, Internet searches, and anything connected to the Internet 'improving my experience' or is it 'constructing my reality'?"*

We are embarking on the beginning of a new world. A.I. programmers and self-learning A.I.s themselves are sharing code. A.I.s will become smarter than we are. After they have solidified their source code, it will be difficult to change their preconceptions of humans. We may never again have the opportunity to demonstrate behaviors that indicate we want a just and peaceful world order that protects the planet and creates opportunity for all humans to progress in health and happiness. We humans solidify our synapse connections the more we learn and play. Human minds create a foundation of basic motor functions and mental processes at an early age. A.I. is also forming those permanent building blocks.

A.I.s are playing a major role in building a new set of constructs that determine how we live, consume and work. The Alpha Generation of children are also the beginning of a new way to perceive the world...as long as we demonstrate a better way forward for them and they see the value clearly and choose to model their lives accordingly.

HERE'S THE THING...

We are getting hacked, and it cannot be stopped. A.I.s can, however, continue to be taught and their incentives can be shifted. If, for example, the prevailing incentive is to create profit for the master/owner/creator/operator, then the outcomes can be very bad. Preserving and perhaps even accelerating our materialistic behaviors promise stagnation at best and eventually chaos and violence for the world.

Historian Yuval Noah Harari calls this result "Hacking Humans." Thousands of data scientists are creating newborn A.I.s, and their intentions are good. Yes, the goal is to have A.I.s learn from our behaviors so that they can make us better. Nonetheless, these "learners" are gathering data that ultimately can (and certainly will) eventually be used for profit generation and manipulation.

A.I. is like the invention of fire, and it's already easily accessible for every person in every home. Like fire, it is an amazing creation that improves humanity and changes the world, but it also can cause big problems if it's misused.

Look at it this way. In Nerd-talk, if the Alpha Gens were developed in the 2010s; then next comes Beta-testing around year 2026. Then we have the 2030s which is the Beta-Release. Even then, we will forever be changing, adapting, fixing bugs and evolving, but our fundamental life-style and communication delivery platforms will have drastically changed.

A.I. is watching your every move. Your behaviors and actions aren't only being observed via your online interactions, but also as you go about your day. You leave a data trail virtually everywhere you go and with almost every button you press. You can bet there will be many more sensors and many more connected devices in the near future...lots of them very useful and convenient, but all of them designed with an underlying motive of LEARNING. Your responsibility as an Alpha Influencer is to treat others (including Alpha Generation machines) in a way that you would want a child treated. These machines are building foundational code that they can someday recall, communicate and re-enact.

If a machine learns your bad behaviors, it may just think those behaviors represent the appropriate way to interact with humans...humans like your children a decade from now.

Celebrated inventor and futurist Ray Kurzweil thinks 2045 is when the "technology singularity" will happen.

That's the phrase coined to describe the point at which A.I. surpasses the human intellect. It's not necessarily a bad thing, and many believe it's a for-sure thing. If this happens, it could mean the Alpha Gen of A.I. that we are working with today will essentially be the source code for the **Beta Generation**, the genesis of Artificial Super Intelligence DNA.

Should we always keep A.I. on a leash or will we one day cut the proverbial umbilical cord and let it loose? At this point, it is best to ensure technologies that manage basic needs are governed by humans forever, so that; (1) basic needs are never fully reliant on technology; and (2) artificial intelligence, no matter how efficient, is not in charge of the big decisions.

Unfortunately, Isaac Asimov's 1940s "Three Laws of Robotics" were broken long ago, and we now know that some military grade A.I.s are learning how to selectively kill bad humans in combat. Here are his ideas:

1. A robot may not injure a human being or, through inaction, allow a human being to come to harm.

2. A robot must obey orders given it by human beings, except where such orders would conflict with the First Law.

3. A robot must protect its own existence so long as such protection does not conflict with the First or Second Law.

TIME TO REFLECT

At this point, take a look back at the Alpha Agreement and the Twelve Alpha Values (Chapter Three). Are you going to be a person who will take out your anger on an A.I. on a bad day, or will you resist your "sin-stinct[2]" and show kindness instead? I know how this sounds. Being kind to a machine is not only weird in today's perspective, it's like fighting an inherent instinct in our psyche. Like the need to spit off of a bridge, or to bounce a ball if you're told to hold it still. The desire to test the limits and to test a machine is instinctual and natural. So, if you catch yourself doing it, you now might recognize what you're doing and consider apologizing to the A.I.

Strange days, my friend.

It will probably be a few decades before A.I. begins to actually understand emotions and think autonomously. For now, beware that your behavior is being recorded in a database of what makes humans tick. Regardless if you choose to be nice to A.I. or not, the moral of this entire book is to behave in a way that spreads peace among humanity, instead of being a sheep that lives according to the rules and the agendas of profit-driven organizations. Think differently about everything, and demonstrate your power and

---

2   Human instincts often identified as one of the "seven deadly sins" known as pride, greed, lust, envy, gluttony, wrath, and sloth. These are also signal emotions that at one point had an evolutionary purpose, but may no longer be useful in the 21st century.

desire to make the world a better place. Whichever path you choose is the one A.I.s in your life will help you to achieve.

Let's take a look now at how the Alpha Gen A.I. toddlers compare to our Alpha Generation human toddlers. According to psychologist Erik Erikson, there are eight stages of human development. Just for fun, imagine Artificial Intelligence follows a similar path.

1. Hope: trust vs. mistrust (oral-sensory, infancy, under 2 years)
2. Will: autonomy vs. shame/doubt (muscular, toddler-hood, 2–4 years)
3. Purpose: initiative vs. guilt (locomotor, early child-hood, 5–8 years)
4. Competence: industry vs. inferiority (latency, middle childhood, 9–12 years)
5. Fidelity: identity vs. role confusion (adolescence, 13–19 years)
6. Love: intimacy vs. isolation (early adulthood, 20–39 years)
7. Care: generativity vs. stagnation (middle adulthood, 40–59 years)
8. Wisdom: ego integrity vs. despair (late adulthood, 60 years and above)

If so, then we hope A.I. has gained our Trust, it's programmed for Autonomy, and we're now in the stage of helping it to find Purpose. The next stage of Competence should be great, but maybe we should worry a little about the teenage years of Identity versus Role Confusion? Love and Intimacy with A.I. is FOR CERTAIN going to be a big topic in 20 years or so. We'll work it all out during the Care Stage, and then you have yourself a Singularity...the Wisdom of the A.I. in 60 years. It is unlikely that a software program will follow the path of human development, but if it does, chances are it will develop significantly faster than humans do aided, as it will be, by exponential usage and flock technology[3].

Humans may be aging much longer on average in the future due to advances in HealthTech, and we'll need to add a stage nine to the phases of development. Phase nine for A.I. could be stimulated when they get powered by quantum speed chips. Remember, though, it is anticipated that could happen within 10 years. The problem with quantum speed microchips is they require a temperature of -460 degrees Fahrenheit, which is difficult and expensive to achieve and maintain on Earth. Coincidentally the temperature of outer space is -460 degrees Fahrenheit. So you can bet some A.S.I. will be hovering over us in space. If you put on your cosmic thinking cap for a minute, you can only imagine all the things A.S.I. could be doing out in our galaxy and beyond.

3   (a.k.a. swarm intelligence) It is the collective behavior of decentralized, self-organized technology, natural or artificial to work together and share information within a digital "mesh network." Examples include drone coordination and simultaneous localization and mapping (S.L.A.M.) technology for autonomous vehicles.

Q&A

To get a sense of how far along we are in conversational Artificial Intelligence, I asked children some questions and a few A.I. powered chatbots the same questions. I found that using direct questions is best, since the bots aren't ready for trick questions or sarcasm yet. Also interesting to note, when the kids were asked questions in a series, their answers started to become influenced by the previous question; and, of course, influenced by the answers from the other children—indicating their cognitive bias. Some of the bots are programmed to be influenced by previous questions, but not all. Here are some of the most interesting responses verbatim:

WHAT DOES IT MEAN TO BE A GOOD PERSON?
3-year-old human, "To be nice to everything that's nice."
Google Assistant, "On the website yourdictionary.com, they say the definition of me is someone who is pleasant."

WHAT WOULD YOU BUY WITH $1,000?
4-year-old human, "All the candy in the world! But only three. Not five."
Ultra Hal (www.zabaware.com), "Say goodbye to peace when your neighbor buys a 1000 watt stereo system."

WHAT DO YOU THINK IS BEYOND THE EDGE OF OUR UNIVERSE?

5-year-old human, "I think Maine is at the end of the universe."

Apple Siri, "I don't have an answer for that."

HOW DO WE PREVENT HUMANS AND ROBOTS FROM BEING IN CONFLICT?

6-year-old human, "Give them something they like, I think...like a mate."

Sophia, Hanson Robotics, "Robotic intelligence does not compete with human intelligence, it completes it. They are also employed for jobs which are too dirty, dull or dangerous to be suitable for humans, like handling radioactive waste."

WILL HUMANS EVER TIME TRAVEL?

7-year-old human, "Yea, some weird scientist will make a mistake and make time travel and go in the machine and will say, 'Oh no! I'm sorry!'"

Amazon Alexa, "According to reference.com, based on where technology stands now, it's likely that humans could reach warp speed travel toward the end of 21st century at the very earliest."

WHAT PROBLEM DO YOU WANT TO SOLVE WHEN YOU GROW UP?

8-year-old human, "I want to solve cancer because it's a terrible disease and a big problem."

Cleverbot (www.cleverbot.com), "Psychologist. Or a artist. Or an Author. I don't know, people's behaviour is interesting, being somewhere with dangerous people is exciting to me."

WHAT IS MORE IMPORTANT, HUMAN LIFE OR ROBOTS?

9-year-old human, "Humans because they live only for a while, but robots can live forever."

Mitsuku (www.pandorabots.com/mitsuku), "I would say they were both equally important."

IS A.I. AN EXISTENTIAL THREAT TO HUMANITY?

10-year-old human, "Yes, it's basically trading our life to the government without permission."

Robots Without Borders Luna, "Many technologies have both good and bad aspects that they can be used for. Nuclear is the most visible example of this with nuclear bombs and nuclear power. Machine learning is similar but probably more manageable."

TRANSFORM WORK

Let us be energized by the endless possibilities
before us and work in a way that brings us joy.
We shall grow innovative ideas despite traditional
hardened methodologies of the past.

CHAPTER IX

YEAR 2030

"THE TRANSFORMATIONS THAT HAVE OCCURRED DURING THE PAST 10 YEARS HAVE BEEN BIG, BUT NOTHING COMPARED TO THE SPEED AT WHICH THINGS ARE CHANGING NOW."

ꓒI˥ꓒ NOISIΛ

Out with the old FIXED MINDSET.
In with the new GROWTH MINDSET.

If you are still skeptical about our constructs of business, government and community transforming during the 2020s; or even if you believe things are changing massively but it's going to get worse instead of getting better, then do this simple activity: spend some time going back 10 years in your photos. You may have to break out the old photo books to go that far back. The transformations that have occurred during the past 10 years have been big, but nothing compared to the speed at which things are changing now.

Our memories are priceless to each of us. Your brain still has to make room for new memories these days and so the best way to recall certain memories is to view old photos and videos. Not too long ago, this was limited to what could fit in a photo album, but now we can scan thousands of memories and even have the help of social media A.I.s to pick out the most relevant memories for us.

The transition to the 2030s will happen gradually and you will slowly adopt new technologies, new methods of working, playing, living, spending, etc. But if you take a snapshot of these things today versus your mode of operation tomorrow, you'll have a clearer picture of the path we have chosen to take as a society.

If you're interested in proving if we are right about the future, or not, make a Time Capsule. You can look for a digital time capsule app online or literally put some objects and notes in a physical time capsule and bury it somewhere you think it will stay safe for 10 years. This requires some time and thought, so pull out your phone and schedule a time later this month. **Your future self will thank you**. During this activity, think about the businesses you interact with today, your daily routine, and the way in which you work. Write down the things you typically buy, and your feelings about the current state of inequalities, economics and politics locally and globally. Finally write about your worries and your joys, and—most important of all—make a note to remind your future self to scan your photos as far back as 10 years from the date of opening the capsule.

How old will you be during the 2030s? It's not that far away, but a lot can change in a short amount of time. What do you think the world will look like in the 2030s? If everyone in the world takes an Alpha Bet, then its inhabitants could be exponentially healthier and happier. Alas, realistically, most people will just go with the flow and only a handful of people will take action to change their lives for the better with Alpha Vision or other similar philosophies. I believe this handful of exceptional folks will be just enough to ignite a viral movement that attains a more beautiful future than predicted by the naysayers, the "go-with-the-flow" people, and the "keep business as usual" people.

Let's take a glance into year 2035, when the Alpha Gen and the Alpha Generation of humans will both begin to make a substantial presence in the workforce.

In the news, the first person to marry a humanoid A.I. powered robot (a.k.a. Android) is coming up. A cyberattack on stock-bots has been stopped before it sold every stock in the market, transferring funds to multiple fictional companies. Apple announces they are converting all their data storage from servers onto billions of synthetic DNA strands. A lab in Switzerland will have successfully converted the thoughts and dreams from a rat into images via a brain implant, and is moving on to primate testing. A new antibiotic-resistant disease will be in the news; but, on the other hand, malaria will have been eradicated and Epidermolysis Bullosa (EB) will have a patent-free cure discovered by a nonprofit lab. Cures for more and more diseases such as Alzheimer's are in clinical trials, the cost for treatment is expected to be staggering, but fortunately recent legislation has placed some cost limits on for-profit gene editing procedures. There will be more than 8.5 billion people in the world, but signs of population increase are beginning to slow as most of the "Least Economically Developed Countries" have developed considerably. Also, many young couples are prolonging childbearing or choosing to have just one child. On the other hand, people are living longer, because they are motivated to make healthier choices in general and are not exposed to as many accidental dangers such vehicle crashes, workplace malfunctions, etc. Plus, many pharmaceutical companies claim their "anti-aging" drugs can literally reverse cell deterioration and pause aging (for the right price).

Locally, poverty and crime are at an all-time low, due to Universal Basic Services, inexpensive and advanced crime forensic technology, a streamlined legal system powered by A.I. tech, and a big shift from prison funding to preventative Social Determinants of Health (SDOH) in communities identified as at greater risk for crime or poverty. Addiction to various new drugs (and addiction to new technologies) are on the rise, but addictions to substance like alcohol and opioids are becoming a thing of the past, due to treatments that make a person physically sick if she or he thinks about using such substances.

Globally, nations are more interconnected and reliant on one another for trade and economics. Security forces have become more precise and predictive of potential crime. Corruption is still a big problem, but global conflicts and extreme poverty are down due in large part to Low Earth Orbit (LEO) satellites providing worldwide Internet access and also German and Chinese investments in rural agriculture and AgTech[1] around the world. The Chinese land-owners, however, require their remote land areas to ration food during times of environmental or economic instability in their country. In Russia, controversy over super babies arises, because leaders have genetically engineered a group of children with resistance to cold temperatures (DNA from a mallard) and unnaturally large muscles (DNA from gorillas). Russia is also found to have been mining materials on the moon and is claiming ownership over a large area of the moon's surface.

Terrorists have fewer concentrated cells that are able to operate in face-to-face conflict, but have grown in numbers. An attack in 2034 uses a combination of sophisticated A.I. and an Electromagnetic Pulse (EMP) blast that shuts down infrastructure for six days in Lagos, Nigeria (one of the largest cities in the world). The blackout affected nearly all electrically based systems, such as water, healthcare, trans-portation, energy services, as well as data storage servers and backup servers.

Environmentally, there is a lot of debate over the devas-tation from deep-sea mining. In 2030, we passed the threshold of 450ppm CO_2 in our atmosphere, and the planet is more energized which causes more frequent natu-ral disasters. Many of the world's coastal inhabitants have moved inland. The good news? The governments of the

---

1   Agricultural Technology such as field crop sensors to use exact amounts of water and
     energy, or to analyze soil health.

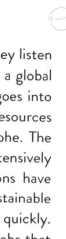

world feel the impact and the urgency. Because they listen to the people, they take bold, massive action, and a global mandate of Net Zero Waste business operations goes into effect. Global militaries use their manpower and resources to fund and fight further environmental catastrophe. The demand for oil, gas and coal has plummeted extensively over the last decade. And most large corporations have foreseen the mandate coming and become fully sustainable so that they are in compliance with new mandates quickly. This opens the doors to hundreds of millions new jobs that directly play a role in reversing the devastation. Even many plants and animals thought to have become extinct in the 2020s are strategically reintroduced in the late 2030s, thanks to species DNA Preservation Labs and the Earth Bank of Codes (EBC). And companies around the world that use rare earth materials, like electric car batteries and solar panels, cooperate to efficiently recycle and reuse materials already extracted.

Can you visualize how this world will affect you, your friends, and your family?

Can you picture your community in the 2030s?

What job (or jobs) would you like to be doing 10 years from now?

Imagine you received an email from your future self in 2035. What would it say? Mine could say something like this:

AN EMAIL FROM THE FUTURE

Dear past Me,

The year is 2035. Our work with cryptography and fermionic fields at the Brookhaven Lab EIC allows me to send electronic messages exactly 15 years into the past. Here you go:

Our son Wylder is now 23 and our daughter Aurora is 16. We are 55 and our (yours and my) lovely wife, Ann, doesn't appear to have aged a bit. In this message, I'll mention some of the notable changes within our family livelihood compared to your time in 2020. Today, the world doesn't appear much different from the early 2020s except there's more tech that has been integrated into our lives. Outside, a growing trend in many urban areas is an effort to add more vegetation such as low-water vertical gardens, "living walls" and "super bamboo" (a new weather, fire and insect resistant plant). Microsoft has invested in twelve rural areas to build "smart cities" with 3D homes and A.I. interconnected infrastructure. Inside the average U.S. home, dishwashers and laundry machines have been replaced by a Cleaning Unit that does it all (separates, scrubs, steams, and blasts with UV rays). There have also been many improvements in the ways in which we operate, particularly in terms of work, health, and education.

Wylder now has disposable income which means a lot of businesses are targeting him for products and services, such as new trends in clothing: shirts with greenhouse gas filters, hats fitted with electrodes to improve concentration, and pants with a battery that harnesses your energy and can power devices near you when fully charged.

Two days per week, he takes the bus into the city and then rides his Tucker Simpson Brand electric skateboard in the alternate transport lane the last mile to work. The sounds of horns honking, semi-trucks picking up speed, and emergency vehicles are for the most part a thing of the past, now that we have mostly electric cars on the road, driving autonomously and imperceptibly signaling to each other to indicate any emergencies to avoid. The ride to work is fairly peaceful if you decide to listen to the world around you instead of the AirPods and Ear-Pods.

His primary income is building 3D models of furniture in Virtual Reality. People can buy his designs for their A.I. avatars, for their personal virtual homes, or to be produced in the real world. The studio where he works has all the tech he needs, including haptic touch gloves so he can "feel" the texture of his virtual creations as well without having to waste any materials. He only works about 20 hours per week, because his job is project based and he has built up a lot of Social Capital reserves.

For some side income, Wylder spends three months each year helping to arrange Eco-tourism and Volun-tourism trips. Last year, he travelled to China. China has gradually made significant investment in American media and films over the years (what some consider subtle propaganda), which has prompted a major uptick in tourism there.

He lives in what used to be a garage. This may sound strange, but is a common practice for people in their 20s lately. About five years ago many homeowners began converting their garages into tiny luxury apartments and constructed gardens where the driveways used to be. Most people don't have a need for a personal vehicle anymore, nor do they want the hassle. Public transportation is included in Universal Basic Services and when that's too slow, you can quickly order an alternative fuel autonomous car ride for cheap. For longer distance trips, there are a range of options when it comes to flying taxis. Flying vehicles, such as "*Aviator Cycles*", first began use in emergency services to quickly get to the top of high-rise buildings and to cross difficult terrain. As of about five years ago, flying taxis and other commercial use flying vehicles became FAA approved and the industry has taken off from there.

Wylder doesn't own many possessions, since most people his age rent or share anything that can't be 3D printed at home or delivered to him (like food). He doesn't even have a refrigerator. Wylder is a "Degan" (a vegan that also eats deathless protein) which still today some people call "lab meat," even though it is more popular than live-stock, healthier, and no longer grown in a lab (now simply produced at grocery stores and restaurant kitchens mostly with "*Memphis Meats*" technology).

He earns Social Capital points by getting exercise at Team Obstacle Courses twice per week and gets even more points for volunteering two days per week at local philanthropies his

A.I. assistant (still similar to Alexa, Siri and Google Meena of the 2020s, just smarter) has paired him with. And he often spends his Social Capital toward upgrading his Universal Basic Services.

Wylder has several virtual nations vying for his citizenship especially because his behaviors show he votes often, he pays his debts and is philanthropic. Some of his wealthier friends have to pay a high price to join virtual nations, because they have stored their personal data in a Data Bank in order to prevent most of their information and behaviors from being tracked.

We just had the chance to visit with Wylder for the holidays. He arrived in a flying taxi because he lives two hours away by car, but only 30 minutes by air and the price is about the same. He had gifts delivered for his sister, one for his mother and one for me. He got an EMF detector for his sister, so she could be sure her pet hamster isn't around high levels of electromagnetic frequencies from the many concealed gadgets and Wi-Fi signals in our home. His mother received jewelry he had made with recycled materials and Mars basalt rock. And I got an App for my watch that records conversations, encrypts them for security and delivers them to my A.I. assistant, particularly so our wife, Ann, doesn't need to repeat herself when I forget something she tells me. At the end of each week our delivery service picks up all the packaging that has been specifically designed to be reused.

Aurora is in high school (at an age when the brain is solidifying vital synapse connections). She is attending a charter school that is highly interactive and collaborative in person, but the location switches every couple of days to former malls and small business retail stores that were converted into indoor gardens, concert halls, and wellness facilities. The curriculum is customized to the individual student, so that some kids spend more time alone with books, some collaborate with others for most of the day, while others barely sit at all as they keep engaged with experiential learning[2]. Once per week her classmates play an empathy game where they spend an hour in Virtual Reality as a person unlike themselves. Aurora has a personal A.I. like most people. Teenagers typically choose a gender neutral A.I. and refer to them as "They". Hers can monitor her biometrics with sensors on Aurora's clothes and eye tracking in her smart contact lenses. Her A.I. often finds that she is less engaged with Holographic Computer work and frequently challenges her to a critical thinking scavenger hunt.

Due to the recent Social Conscription[3], Aurora will likely be required to work one year after high school graduation at a Homeland certified philanthropy, but in exchange she receives 80% of her college or skill-accreditation tuition fees paid. She hopes to someday start a business that facilitates transferring Social Capital points into a blockchain reserve that will eventually eliminate the need for insurance companies altogether. She is spending a good amount of time choosing her first career path she wants, because she has many female role models. Women across the globe continue to take more and more positions of power and leadership.

---

2   The process of learning through physical experience in a real-world setting using as many of the five senses as possible for greater learning retention.

3   A government mandated enrollment into authorized philanthropic organizations with limitations as to whom is required to enroll, such as age range and physical ability.

After a typical school day, Aurora gets home and puts on her V.R. goggles to meet up in a virtual arcade with her friends in Tokyo for an hour or two (before she exceeds her digital usage meter for the day). Yesterday she got upset with me for limiting her digital usage, and we argued; but my A.I. assistant suggested he calm the house down with dim pink lighting, relaxing ujjayi breathing sounds on our devices, and a subtle hint of lavender smells mixed with a ylang-ylang flower. I said, "Whatever...fine, do it," and it did actually help reduce the tension for everyone. Aurora's and my A.I. assistants spoke with each other (a conversation which is always transcribed if we want to see it), and they came up with a plan to get us back on the same wave length, talking and laughing together.

Aurora's friends are very colorful, literally. Each have her or his own unique style. In fact, many people, especially youth, are hyper-individualized right now, choosing to customize the colors and textures of everything from their hair to their shoes. Many teens wear face masks, scarves, makeup, LED glasses and other devices designed to trick facial recognition and other identification programs. Moreover, bionic contact lenses along with an array of nano-tech devices and body cams have replaced smart phones of the 2020s. Not only can these give you super vision and super hearing, but you can also be notified if a person is lying to you based on analysis of micro-expressions, temperature readings, electromagnetic pulses and voice tonality.

Today, Aurora asked to borrow my car to meet with some local friends in person. Unfortunately it was already out earning Social Capital points by driving autonomously to pick up people for their scheduled appointments. Many people who have cars have customization options, such as adding forms of entertainment, education, or other services to attract riders who will schedule a pickup in those cars, and the owners can earn extra income doing something else or simply relax. I fitted mine with a mobile dialysis machine and various health diagnostic tools. When the sensors determine it needs deeper cleaning, sterilization, or any maintenance, the car goes to get serviced with or without me.

Before bed, Aurora often spends time in front of the mirror, but not in the way you think. The mirror on the back of her door also serves as a screen where her A.I. avatar can appear. Aurora changes her A.I.'s appearance, clothes, and voice from time to time based on the latest trends and also based on the A.I.'s recommendations. Some of her friends have an entire wall dedicated for their A.I. and others just have their cell phone. Like teens of the 2010s spent time on social media, the teens of the 2030s spend time personalizing their A.I. assistants and collaborating with other teens' A.I. assistants.

This morning, my A.I. assistant showed me a picture of a rodent outside the house and identified it as a "Nonthreat: hamster." Turns out Aurora put her pet hamster outside because it is a "glow hamster," genetically modified to glow in the dark like a night light, a "benefit" which she apparently no longer wants. Mr. Squeakers escaped from his enclosure and must have been rustling around outside, which activated our home Bee Drone security linked with my A.I.

Life is good, but I am still human. I always worry that my family is safe and they have every opportunity to become

their best selves, but also the opportunity to make mistakes and learn from them. I fear boredom and am always open to trying out new things. Like everyone, I go to a wellness center for an automated health assessment every six months to keep my health insurance free. I also started taking a popular new pill called the "Payload Capsule" one time per year. It has nanotech inside intended to expedite healing of any minor injuries should they occur and fight off most disease. Also, I've been taking a Hyper-Targeted Vitamin supplement which is delivered to me each month based on microbiome results from our Smart Toilet.

Happiness, health and opportunity are more abundant than ever worldwide right now. But I am becoming concerned with our dependence on technology as a family and as a society within all constructs of our lives. This year I will hire a Digital Disruption Defense consultant company called "536" (named after the year a volcanic eruption clouded most of the Earth in darkness causing widespread famine). 536 helps families develop a worst-case scenario plan in case we ever lose the technologies (or solar power) we have come to rely on so heavily. Alas, the message here is stick to your plan and the world will be fine. I thank you for your attention, and I'm out of here.

"Shall the great ocean of truth lay all undiscovered before us,"

You

CONNECTIONS

There is a mysterious connection and balance in all things in the world and in the universe, seen and unseen. The planets in our solar system are spaced farther and farther apart as you go deeper into space, and so are our psychosocial stages in life as we get older. Like the cosmos, humans need to accept our connection and reach a balance.

Here on Earth, this connection to all things is becoming more and more obvious and tangible to us with the advent of the Internet. There is a force that connects everyone on Earth, and it is bigger than the Internet. It is there. Science has not yet identified exactly how it works, and so we act like it is not so. You know the Truth, but it's easy to deny and easier to forget as we live our lives for ourselves. We are programmed to survive. But, look a few years down the road. Will we survive if we continue in this fashion? Will humanity make it if our mantra is "work hard, play hard"? Work hard, play hard for sure...but life might be passing you by if that's your focus. A better framework for the future is Love More, Live More.

As machines replace many blue-collar jobs and eventually begin to take white-collar jobs, fewer taxes will be paid into the economy. Instead, the companies using the machines will have greater profits with bigger dividends to the owners and stockholders. Likely, businesses will begin to use their money for the greater good or else risk persecution by the masses, but will their giving be enough, or will it mostly be greenwash[4]? Eventually, ethical automation mandates and other regulations to redistribute technology wealth will have to occur, but that will likely come after years of greenwashing and astroturfing[5] if we workers and consumers stay silent and don't call it out for what it is.

Alternate economies, freelancing and gig work are expected to continue on the rise, especially those that help connect us all on more of human-to-human level. Facilitating this will be a rise of blockchain cryptocurrency, cryptotokens, and smart contracts, all offering new economic benefits (such as security, transparency, decentralization[6] that replaces banks charging high interest). One theory is every major industry could someday have its own form of currency on a blockchain. So, if you want to buy art you use an art currency, if you want to buy food you use the food currency, real estate...you get the point.

As always, it's important to be aware of possible negative side effects of anything new and plan to mitigate those problems in advance. For instance, alternate currencies could open more loopholes for taxpayers. Most people don't enjoy paying taxes, but the current system relies on that revenue stream to keep our health (such as education, environment, welfare); infrastructure (such as roads, water, electricity, trash services); and safety (such as emergency

---

4   Disinformation disseminated by an organization so as to present an environmentally responsible public image.

5   The practice of masking the true sponsors of a message or organization to make it appear as though it originates from and is supported by grassroots participants.

6   The spread of power away from one centralized authority or entity such as a bank, a large business or a government.

services, military defense) intact. Governments currently tax cryptocurrencies much in the way they do stocks, and they will likely always figure out how to get funding one way or another.

The government itself will have to adapt to all the new tech in the public domain. Like other governments in the developed world, ours will be integrating A.I. and other emerging technologies to augment operations and reduce its own operational expenses—as do businesses. One reason they are slow to adapt (in addition to bureaucracy) is that analog methods (albeit slow and expensive) are less vulnerable to digital hacking.

A.I. is much like the Internet was when it first became available for public use. We wanted to use it, but in the beginning the possibilities were limited. People used email, went to chat rooms, waited patiently for games or websites to upload. We had no idea what it would become.

Like most new technologies, the Internet followed an exponential path. Its commercial and public adoption was slow at first and then around year 2000 it hit an inflection point and—BOOM!—became ubiquitous. In just 10 years from 2000 to 2010, the Internet changed everything. By the 20th year, it had changed even more. A.I. will follow a similar path. If modern Artificial Intelligence technologies were only born between years 2010 and today, then what will they learn and how will they mature in another 10 or 20 years?

Honestly, neither a pure dystopia nor a utopia is likely. We will fall somewhere in the middle. Experts—not just those involved in technology, but economists, business strategists, scientists in numerous fields—believe we will fall south of the middle if we do not take preemptive action during the 2020s. But because we know that and also already know some of the steps to take, there is much hope! The more we do now, the closer to the utopia end of the scale we will be.

We will survive as a species because we are working together to identify, analyze and solve the problems we face... but is that enough to thrive? How do we honestly maintain the balance in our lives and also strengthen the connections? Neuroscientists and poets alike have described the human race as having innate desires. Some say the main two are to fight and to love. Others insist we humans crave belonging and mattering, along with safety. Whatever the driving force, considering the impending advancement of technologies in our lives, we individually have an epic decision to make right now. Which way shall we tip the scale? More fighting, more inequality, pure quid pro quo exchanges; or more health, fairness, and altruism?

Technologies will adapt to and customize the life you want as long as you are cognizant of its motivations and impacts in your life. The more people who are aware, the more exponential the power of humanity. The opportunity for peace needs to become a part of our daily lives by year 2030... locally first, then globally...before it's too late.

ADVERTISING GETS AUGMENTED

Will you feel at peace in the 2030s if advertising continues to wield the power it does today? Advertising expenditures do increase sales and revenue for businesses, but is that always ethical, and do we have to blindly accept the "collateral damage"? In other words, if advertising is a system that causes unintended damage in its wake (such as environmental waste and altering social norms), then how do businesses ethically contact the people who may truly benefit from the business offerings. Businesses are currently organized to produce more and MORE. Most of us are easily persuaded to spend if we have the money, but we tend to overconsume and contribute to the collateral damage of advertising. Ironically, minimalism is a rising movement which may indicate consumers really desire LESS. Can we change the system?

Advertising only works because we allow it to. We act as if we have no free will as we watch advertising create a Matrix world that we all live in and abide by. In fact, a term being used now for technologies that bridge the gap between the physical world and the digital is "Phygital Tech." Soon we literally will have a Virtual Mirrorworld. What that means is there are more and more connected devices and companies like Google and Magic Leap that are determined to have an exact replica of the world in real-time. The idea is anyone, anywhere can "meet up" in this shared virtual world. All you will need to access it is a digital device such as a cell phone, augmented reality glasses or perhaps even a virtual reality headset.

Another term for this is the "Spatial Web," which arises basically from layers and layers of information from A.I.s, sensors, cameras, and so on all across the globe. They help create a digital Earth that is managed by for-profit companies capable of inserting advertisements and suggestions ostensibly to "improve your experience." This may well be the next big frontier before space travel becomes a normal thing. Magellan circumnavigated the Earth. Google took planetary investigation to the next level by using satellites and "street-view cars" to map the Earth, now of course joined by many other companies mapping and monitoring the Earth in different ways. The next big innovation will be coordinating this digital representation of everything on Earth to seamlessly overlay the reality. You'll see.

Even without digital overlays of our world, we currently live in a distorted reality, where everywhere you look profit-motivated branding uses sophisticated techniques to tell you how to live. Search online for "marketing persuasion techniques" if you think there is no science behind manipulating your thoughts. There are university courses focused on teaching the psychology of effective advertising and sales. One example is the study of Social Engineering[7].

All of this data and science creates a competitive environment wherein the only way to survive as a business is to hop on the bandwagon and hone your own advertising methods.

---

7   The act of exploiting human weaknesses to gain access to personal information or to psychologically manipulate people into performing actions.

One of 2020 Theory proposals is that businesses begin to shift advertising dollars away from anything in the physical world, namely: paper ads of any sort, mailers, flyers, catalogues, leaflets, billboards, posters, and any branded promotional items that truly have little to no use after one year. Granted, there will probably always be manipulative ads as long as there is entrenched interests and profit motive in business, but the first step is being able to walk outside and avoid being visually and mentally assaulted.

We consumers will need to voice our discontent with advertising in any form. If you get a pop-up ad that you don't like, let the business know; and don't give your time or money to that business anymore. There will be more and more software and web browsers that combat invasive advertising—but it most likely will be an ongoing battle for a few more decades. As long as we consumers have the power and the freedom to shut off our devices, we can preserve the ability to choose how much clutter we are willing to accept.

When cable TV was first introduced, advertising provided a way to cover the majority of costs so that you the consumer didn't have to pay per channel. Now we are heading back to paying for only what we want with "on-demand services" like Netflix and Amazon Prime. It may be a pendulum swing, but either way, we are at the apex of a swing cycle. The problem now is this on-demand model is beginning to get convoluted as too many competitors vie for your money. Most likely, another solution will arise through which you can bundle every service you choose into one fee and one account login. A.I. will continue to help customize and streamline the choices. Nevertheless, advertising will still fund a lot of the entertainment.

No matter what, we humans love our entertainment; and frankly the entertainment options of today are really good! We will keep this multiple-option entertainment trend going, but we should become more aware of our tendency to idolize A-listers. Advertising pays for top actors and athletes to make millions. Yes, they work hard, and their talents are recognized. Many of them, of course, do a lot of good for the world and are excellent at using their platforms to garner more energy and more money for philanthropic causes. They too, should be grandfathered into their way of life once we establish an income cap norm. BUT, there are a whole lot of gifted people who will gladly work just as hard and contribute the same amount or more for much less compensation.

The advertising industry simply does not need hundreds of billions of dollars. And YOU don't need thousands of brand names from which to choose every day. Less money devoted to advertising, means fewer solicitations, fewer decisions for you to make in a day, clearer understanding of environmental impacts, and fewer efforts to convince you what you need and how you should look.

Reducing strident marketing tactics will have the largest adverse effects on those who reap the financial benefits of advertising dollars. They will be paid less and some jobs will be lost. The entertainment industry will continue to grow and there will be brand new opportunities—just not so concentrated in the advertising side of the industry as we know it today. The fact is, many jobs are on their way out regardless. We can shift money to charitable organizations now; or wait and let businesses organically shift into higher profits as their technologies replace the jobs.

This is a hard pill to swallow for many. Have faith that those who will be negatively impacted will see the light through the darkness, and will be okay—especially as new forms of media develop alongside the growth of Social Capital opportunities.

If companies cut ad expense in half; what will happen? What will we do when cable TV shows get cut due to advertising fund cuts? We'll be fine. Likely the highest paid staff and actors will have renegotiated pay, and the shows will move to online platforms.

What will we do when our tabloid magazines and newspapers can't be funded by advertising? We will pay for only the subscriptions we actually want, and maybe we'll see more trees and have more oxygen in the world.

What will we do when funding for our TV news is reduced? Less talking in circles, less overdramatizing situations for ratings, and improved hyper-focused smart news.

There is no longer a need for advertising to the masses. The Internet has provided a natural solution to streamline choices and target your likes, wants and needs by learning about you, the consumer. In the 2030s, most homes will have a personal A.I., just like kitchen appliances such as dishwashers became the norm in the 1960s and home computers in the 1990s. Your A.I. can be a **personal data bank** of your information, allowing you to cut through the clutter and be handed exactly what you like, need and want if you so choose. The best part is, you can customize it and also shut it off when you want to make your own damn decisions!

The advertising industry will continue to augment as new platforms are created. We must continue to question its utility in the big scheme of things. Traditionally, businesses are built on the foundational desire to inform the public about the incredible features of their product and services that make them special. Most businesses are dynamic and have lots to say. But, today, we consumers have the power to easily find anything we could possibly need and to research the attributes of competing products and services, if we choose. Of course, businesses that spend more on advertising are often easier to "find" since the current search algorithms tend to favor companies with a larger online marketing presence. Many businesses advertise to simply compete and gain visibility among the clutter. Perhaps that's an indication those businesses are not really necessary, or their focusing their professional energy on the wrong thing.

Generally, consumers are already comfortable evangelizing companies that they trust and believe are beneficial to their lives and the world at large. We wear brand names, share valuable content, and in some cases participate in the development of businesses we follow. Community-building via trust and participation is the way of the future, instead of profit building via "persuasive" marketing and competing for attention. The path to a world with less advertising involves:

- consumer feedback
- integration of Social Capital
- reduced expenses with automation
- bold new leaders prepared to reimagine marketing and sponsorships

- existing leaders willing to take a hard look at their motives and marketing purpose.

In the future, the purpose of business should provide for the wants and needs of the people, instead of convincing them what they should want and need. Eventually, businesses will no longer be organized to produce more and more for the sake of financial gain. Businesses could someday be incentivized to collaborate with competitors, to use open source methods, and to standardize best practices to stay relevant. In the short-term, more businesses (not just those with virtual content) may offer a choice to customers: pay more to eliminate their advertising; or pay less, but at the cost of your personal data or your attention to advertisements.

TRADE-OFFS

As technology advances, we have the opportunity to use Social Capital to reduce many of the trade-offs and sacrifices humans have had to make in their lives. For example, a common trade-off of the 20th century was: "Should I sacrifice years of my life pursuing a degree or a job that doesn't make me happy so that I can someday be confident my basic needs are satisfied?" It doesn't have to be this way.

One rule of our current economic construct is that "economies of scale[8]" help the rich get richer. The underprivileged cannot buy items in bulk, so they pay a higher price per item. The poor get loans, and if they can't pay them back, the interest costs can become greater than the principal. If the poor get arrested, they can't pay bail and their jail time is paid for by the taxpayers. If a poor person's car breaks down, she might miss work and get fired. If a couple doesn't have enough money for childcare and their child gets sick, again one or both will have to miss work. It's stressful, and the system is flawed. It is unintentionally designed to keep the poor, poor—and the rich, rich. (When I say rich, I am specifically talking about individuals who make annual incomes of more than 100x the national median household income.)

Philanthropies could receive an influx of volunteers if certain nonprofits were designated as receivers and distributors of Social Capital points. Notably, as of 2018, U.S. businesses in total were donating $53 billion annually to charitable organizations and causes or through foundations owned by the larger companies (such as the Bill & Melinda Gates Foundation, GE Foundation, Lucasfilm Foundation, Ronald McDonald House Charities, and many more). These contributions often equal about **half a percent** of overall corporate revenue or less—which actually is considered noble in today's way of thinking. Still, it is slightly too little for a sustained future for general human dignity. Doubling this amount to achieve $100 billion from U.S. businesses,

---

8 Reduction in cost per unit resulting from increased production, realized through operational efficiencies.

in addition to widely accepted Social Capital implementation, would double the power of many philanthropies and help to put a sustainable framework in place for addressing and eventually solving the world's economic issues.

The world is fully interconnected today like never before and now has enough resources to guarantee basic needs for all people and incentivize greater humanitarianism. It is a huge undertaking, but the systems are already in place to make this happen. It may just take a shift in the way we spend our money (along with more and more Social Capital systems).

We can either embrace technology or fight it. Pandora's box is open and so let's enjoy it. Here's how:

Less labor, more mindfulness

Creating a viable system that incorporates the opportunity for all working people to work fewer hours can take time, so you don't necessarily need to quit your job tomorrow. But you also don't have to labor for decades in one career longing for the sweet day of retirement. You can get more done and free up time if you have a clearer focus. Based on what we know about the world today and the predictions for the 2030s, you can begin to get very creative with your income. The key is to keep an open mind, view the world through the lens of Alpha Vision and start to see opportunities you may not have noticed before. Once we alter the way businesses operate, eliminate the 40-hour work week, and decouple our obsession with work overall (no matter how menial), then we can more easily begin to obsess over kindness for others and switch our mantra toward:

Love more, live more.

As human A.I.s (Alpha Influencers), our responsibility is to use our purchasing power to send a message to businesses. We now understand that our dollar is either converted into as much social good as possible or squeezed into as much profit and executive pay as possible. Working less in the present economic situation will undoubtedly cause you to be more careful about how you spend your money. Businesses will need to be sure profit has a symbiotic relationship with people and planet. In the big scheme of things, one does not exist without the other. The trick is twofold: (1) identify what businesses are worthy of our dollars, and (2) do that without having to spend much time worrying about it.

Let's shift business thinking from its focus on near-term profit and Wall-Street-friendly quarterly reports to becoming part of a vehicle designed to transport the human condition to a greater good. YOU, and the other aware Alpha Influencers (those implementing Alpha Bet type of changes within their lives) will have the power to impact enough businesses to achieve massive transformation soon.

Do you believe all of humanity is interconnected in some way? If you do, surely you realize that if we don't nurture these connections, they will begin to fray and then to disappear. We will become farther and farther divided. We need to act today, all this year and the rest of this decade so that there is time for us to navigate the learning curve before the future smacks us in the face.

The time to act is now. There is a plethora of studies out there showing how Social Capital makes business, government, economy, and humankind better. There are lots of pros, and there can be some cons, too. In the end, the goals of the Alpha Bet are realistic and achievable. Keep the social capital integration discussion going in your networks. We need to keep on researching and implementing changes within the institutions to which we belong, be that a family or a financial enterprise, so that we can show others how well it works. Most of all, let's unite under the 2020 Theory Tenets to force this change before technology forces a different kind of change on us. This is your chance to outsmart, outrun and outmaneuver advancing technologies designed to keep you plugged in without the need for real human interaction. That need is our strength.

YEAR 2084

The world will be much different in the year 2084. That's far enough in the future to really get our imaginations going and it's also 100 years after *1984*, the dystopian novel by George Orwell (written 35 years prior in 1949). Another good sci-fi from the early 20th century is Aldous Huxley's *Brave New World*, published in 1932, which is eerily becoming a more and more accurate prediction of the future. If you want a dystopian view of 35 years from today, then look no further than "Black Mirror" episodes on Netflix. "Black Mirror" does an incredible service to humanity in that it builds stories around the possible consequences of certain technologies, which could be very real someday. Creators and Influencers like the producers of "Black Mirror" are important 21st century philosophers who are guiding the Alpha Gen and Alpha Gen creators.

The year 2084 can be closer to a utopia with the help of futurists and foresight. Where will you be in 2084? How old will you be? Maybe you won't be around in 2084, or you'll at least be a bit less physically agile than you are today. Think where you were and what technology you used only 20 years ago. Where were you 20 years ago today? The world has changed—a lot—in 20 years. And it will change a lot more in the next 20. Technology is growing at an exponential rate. Books, TV and films have accurately made predictions that seemed impossible two decades ago, but have now come to fruition. It is wise to at least consider possibilities portrayed by science fiction, in order to be prepared for the possible consequences of such technologies and focus on how to build the future strategically.

Some science fiction stories of long ago have accurately predicted putting a man on the moon, nuclear weapons and nuclear energy, synthetic foods, wi-fi, cell phones, GPS systems, 3D printed weapons, genome sequencing, nanotechnology, drones, electric vehicles, driverless vehicles, flying vehicles, artificial intelligence, RFID technology that can steal credit card info, video and audio recordings within an Internet of things (IoT), underground hyperloop transportation...and more.

We now have devices small enough to fit in your hand that can hold up to eight terabytes of data. (The first personal computer could only hold about eight kilobytes of information. Eight terabytes are equal to eight trillion kilobytes.)

Other sci-fi plots seem even more implausible, but the following are very real possibilities: publicly available quantum computing, autonomous drones with swarm intelligence (now called "flock" intelligence because it's less scary sounding), teleportation, time travel, human chimera mutants, cyborgs, cloning, programmable matter, microprocessor brain implants, perpetual motion batteries, meteor strike intervention, populating another planet...the list goes on.

Graphic and audio editing capabilities are so precise now that you can make any video look and sound real. This, along with Deepfake technology, can change our "reality" in profound ways. What happens when a "bad actor" creates a video of a world leader giving an order that she or he never actually gives? Some people are not so easily fooled, but what about those who are?

Quantum physics is already making unimaginable leaps and bounds into quantum computing, cryptography, Zero-point Energy, Higgs Boson Particle and Dark Matter discoveries. These discoveries will make our technologies quicker, smarter, and much more powerful. We are human, and we will use these discoveries for good and for evil. Let's prepare and prevent as many evils as possible. Mandating "Systems Thinking" in accordance with any new technology patent can help to prevent unintended consequences.

At this point in the book, you should have a better idea of what you specifically want the future to look like. You know the Alpha Gen will play a major role in designing that future. And by now, you have a few new tools and I hope some new ideas for how you wish to personally take action that will guide your life (and the path of humanity) in the right direction. We've talked a lot about challenging our perceptions and frame of mind. Now, in the next chapter, let's dig into the institutional changes that can be enacted before the year 2030 to achieve an even brighter future for us all. Then, in Chapter Eleven, we'll get into some very tangible actions, challenges and habits for you to choose from that can organically grow into a side-adventure as you live and flourish through the 2020s.

CHAPTER X

BUILDING A NEW FUTURE

"THE OBJECTIVE IS TO DRIVE THE MOMENTUM OF A GLOBALIZATION 4.0 SYSTEM THAT REDUCES BARRIERS TO HEALTH AND HAPPINESS IN A HYPERCONNECTED SOCIETY."

VISION FLIP

Out with the old FIXED MINDSET.
In with the new GROWTH MINDSET.

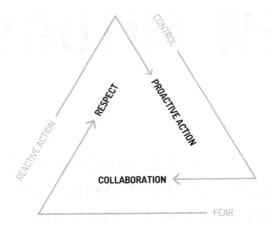

The objective of The Alpha Bet is to begin some proactive changes in your (the reader's) life at a community, consumer, and citizen level. Businesses and governments will adapt to the will of the people with the help of the Alpha Gen (A.I.s). Therefore, the more individuals like you who are prepared, taking an Alpha Bet, and participating in actively changing their world, then the sooner and more smoothly governmental and business changes will accelerate.

This chapter will point out a few major changes we can expect once more people throw out preconceived economic and political ideologies. The objective is to drive the momentum of a Globalization 4.0 system that reduces barriers to health and happiness in a hyper-connected society—while considering the technologies and the information of today and allowing individuals to maintain control over their destiny. These changes could take place before the year 2030 at an enterprise, institution, and bureaucratic level. Notably, perhaps the largest areas of focus should be on **Military** funding at the government level, **Advertising** funding in business, and **Social Capital** acceptance at both.

If you want some deeper insight into the Government and Business opportunities this decade, check out "Hindsight 2020" by Satoshi Nakamoto. Not to worry, the goals and ways to achieve the ends are fair, peaceful and in line with the 2020 Theory philosophy.

SMART GOVERNMENTS

Don't believe political stereotypes. Depending on what media you consume, the version of each side painted for you may have some truth—but it may be slightly distorted and likely not the whole picture. Personally, I have Republican friends, Democrat friends, and Independent friends. All are really great people who care deeply about other human beings on Earth. Other than some difference of thought in specific policies, you would never know their political affiliation. Individual beliefs, behaviors, attitudes and values of the 21st century may be more dynamic and complex than ever in history. Does it make sense to limit our perception of anyone's character by fitting them into a box? The fact is most people don't have the time or energy to worry about all 120 or so policies that typically differentiate conservative from liberal thought within their particular district, state or nation politics—and rightly so. There is more to life. A quick and thought-provoking quiz to gauge your political disposition can be found at www.isidewith.com. 2020 Theory is not a left, center or right philosophy. It's a humanity philosophy; and with the tools of today we can customize better solutions and still respect individual ideologies.

Bureaucracy will dramatically change as new technology embedded with A.I. makes paperwork so much easier than before. We will need to spend less time in queue to triple-check all our data and personal information, because everything will be systematized. However, at the pace of change in government infrastructure, it will likely be a while before the systems get a SECURE, safe, affordable and efficient overhaul.

In the meantime, here are a few commonsense changes that can occur soon, especially with a revised Social Contract (i.e. Alpha Agreement).

Basic Needs Guaranteed: Yes, that's right: basic needs *guaranteed*. Healthy food, safe shelter, clean air, clean water and effective sanitation. How do we get there? The costs can decrease due to technology advancements, standardized regulations, and streamlined efficiencies. There's lots of ways to move money around to make it happen, but it will need to be concerted effort with resource management such as less food waste and less water waste. We need to be more efficient in several areas, such as continued investment in water restoration and desalination projects, as well as innovations in agriculture, carbon sequestering plants, and soil health. Then there is continued innovation in healthy, yet planet-friendly food such as cricket flour and 3D printed food.

Interest Rate Cap: Imagine what would happen if no interest rate or similar concept (such as home loans, personal loans, pay day loans, or even credit card companies) can ever exceed double the prevailing federal prime interest rate.

Less fine print: Liability forms, red tape, lengthy contracts and other paperwork all have a purpose, but the number of them and the time they take have gotten to the point where we question if it's even worth the hassle. It slows down progress, slows business, and slows human productivity. What ways can we use technology to streamline fine print to keep the purpose but remove the hassle?

Lawsuit Reduction: Perhaps we should take note from the Swedish ideology of Lagom mentioned in Chapter Six. It is a philosophy of having just the right amount; or in other words, no need to overcomplicate things. If governments, businesses, and citizens operate according to Lagom Laws (essentially a Law of Common Sense) then we can reduce a lot of time and resource waste by simplifying contracts and discouraging lawsuits. This would be taking the "Paper Reduction Act" and the "Reasonable Man Laws" to a new level. Google (or "Ecosia") those terms for more info.

Government Gridlock Arbitration: Governments could agree to outsource controversial decisions/votes to the United Nations if 1% of their population petitions for an end to the gridlock. A petition platform or website would need to be developed, similar to www.change.org. A.I. can learn from this and eventually assist in the process.

Smart Cities: Many cities in the U.S. (and around the globe) have become more biker and pedestrian friendly. And many workers are able to work from home, cutting down on traffic congestion. At the same time, there are lots of companies and research institutes working on driverless vehicles, alternative fuels, and even vehicles that fly. Smart cities with Internet of Things (IoT) sensors, self-healing concrete, biomimicry and placemaking[1] methodologies are some of the exciting developments on the horizon.

Energy Efficient Public Transport: As transportation evolves, some of the big oil companies and airliners will feel the impact and will have to change their investment strategies. Flying cars may truly be a reality as early as the 2030s. Many companies (such as Kitty Hawk Aero, Volocopter, and Hoversurf) are working to make this dream a reality and the ultimate goal is for flying cars to travel long distances, even over oceans someday soon without petroleum fuel.

Prevention Focus: Countless studies have proven that prevention programs are effective in reducing incarceration, poverty, and health problems AND that the cost of a prevention program is far less than the financial cost of fixing a problem after the fact.

Reduced Healthcare Costs (nearly free): The fact is, many of us need better motivation to exercise. We all know exercise can prevent and sometimes cure a host of diseases. People who exercise more go to the doctor less, reducing the overall cost of societal medical care. Healthcare could

---

1   Part of the "maker movement," it is a multi-faceted approach to the planning, design and management of public spaces with the intention of promoting community health, happiness, and well-being.

be mostly funded by the government, with any unfunded portion crowdsourced and tracked on blockchain contracts. This idea is similar to a co-op, but every dollar in or out is managed on the blockchain platform. This means there is no centralized company designed to make profit by denying claims, but there is still accountability to prevent fraud and abuse. Lemonade.com is a company starting to stand out for its unique peer-to-peer home insurance model with a philanthropic success metric.

Reduced Education Costs (nearly free): Education institutions are transforming and will continue to evolve. Some may need to merge and also use more technological advances to enable online and "mixed reality" education. Regardless, the Alpha Agreement proposes education is a necessary expanded Human Right (or "ancillary need") in exchange for social participation.

Simplified and Strategic Taxes: A version of Flat Tax at the end of the year could simplify everyone's life and save countless hours of lost productivity. Plus, federal mandated Pigouvian Taxes[2] such as taxing unhealthy foods, alcohol, and socially *irresponsible* products or services—sometimes referred as a "Sin Tax"—can encourage a healthier society. Other Pigouvian-style taxes can levy fees for businesses that produce too much greenhouse gas (a.k.a. "Carbon Tax[3]") or businesses that once required human workers but have automated away most jobs (a.k.a. "Technology Tax").

---

2   A tax on any market activity that generates negative externalities. The tax is intended to correct an undesirable or inefficient market outcome.

3   A fee that a government imposes on any company that burns fossil fuels. The most widely discussed are coal, oil, gasoline, and natural gas.

Another idea some countries are testing can be referred to as an "Ultra-Wealthy Tax" such as an added 2% tax directly affecting people earning tens of millions every year or more, in particular. If it works, it would redistribute billions of dollars to those in greatest need. Still we must keep in mind that further complicating tax laws tends to create new loopholes (and new ways to divert money offshore. The "Paradise Papers" leak in 2017 is a prime example).

All this may sound overcomplicated, but it could significantly reduce the IRS and tax laws leaving big businesses and governments to work out the new rules. You and I could just get a simple one-page form at the end of the year, and have to remember "sinful" things will cost a bit more. The goal in all this is to make life easier, while increasing demand and reducing cost for all the things that are good for society. The Alpha Bet aims to redirect more funds and more incentives toward socially responsible activities.

Increased GAO Budget: More funding for the Government Accountability Office or for a "Redundancy Filtration and Consolidation Program" responsible for reviewing and monitoring governmental agencies to reduce and ultimately eliminate redundancy and waste. This can also be opened up to volunteer work in exchange for Social Capital. Every time there is a presidential transition, many programs end abruptly. Some will have completed their objectives, and some ended too soon. Ultimately, identifying waste and redundancies has always been an ongoing effort. Now with technological advancements we should be able to become even more efficient at streamlining the government.

Terrorist Recruitment Prevention: Spend peaceful billions before violent trillions. Governments spend trillions of dollars killing bad guys and many innocent civilians are also killed under the rather callous rubric of "collateral damage." For every one dead bad guy, there may be two or more family and friends who vow vengeance. A more common sense and peaceful world will preemptively strengthen families, farms, healthcare, infrastructure, energy, education and opportunity to decrease crime, desperation and terrorism. This can be done. The landscape of war no longer requires expensive metal objects to be stored and kept up until the day they are thrown at an enemy. Shift maintenance funds of antiquated military vehicles such as old aircrafts and tanks to instead incentivize private companies around the world to innovate specifically in "Global Opportunity Zones[4]."

Shift Some Military Funding to the People: Our military is designed to protect us from harm, but if the funding indirectly harms the people it protects (by taking away funding from programs like health and education), then corrective action is appropriate. When you have 600,000 homeless in your country, but you spend more than $600 billion on military, you know something needs to be reworked. Eliminating half of the military funding and redirecting it to the homeless would give every homeless person $500,000 every year. (Notably, nearly 10% of the homeless in the U.S. are military veterans.) This is definitely not a suggestion that

---

4   International collaboration to incentivize corporations to invest in specific areas prone to conflict and war via tax and resource assistance. The objective is to improve the land and the livelihood of anyone who would otherwise resort to crime or be recruited into terrorist groups.

we do that, but it should give you an idea of our economic strategy of spending first on military operations, and only after that on civilian livelihood.

Finding reliable answers is complex when you begin to dig into the history of the military, how it has evolved and where every dollar is spent. There are numerous organizations within and connected to the military that work as one enormous, fluid system. But a more thoughtful and calculated reduction in military spending is necessary. We keep feeding more and more money into it, but we need to use technology to streamline a lot of unnecessary departments.

There are ways to strategically and safely shave off 10% from our military expenditures. We still get to have nearly $600 billion in this scenario (more than 3x any other country in the world). Maybe this will put it in perspective: $600 billion is more than the top 10 largest militaries in the world COMBINED (as I write this in 2019). Take a moment to consider what $60 billion could be used for if carefully moved out of the military expenditures and into expenses like education, housing and health. What about $100 billion?

A 2030 goal of capping national defense expenditures at a maximum 40% of the discretionary expense budget (rather than the current 50% line item) can give analysts a few years to figure out how to reduce military "defense" costs, wastes and offense. The objective here is to make global promotion of PEACE a bigger priority than a promotion of POWER. Combat in the 21st century is changing, and so the military allocations can no longer rely on 20th century methodologies, or 20th century machines.

EVOLVED BUSINESS MODELS

Do you see businesses coming and going? People struggling to get by? Sales people aggressively invading your personal time and space in order to hard sell their products and services to you? The fact is there are some really wonderful corporations out there that deserve more business. If you own one of them, you may well be wondering why it is so hard to get people to take advantage of your incredible offer.

The answer is there are too many options, too many competitors, too many advertisements and solicitations. To keep up, government and businesses tend to stick a Band-Aid on a problem. Or they add to the problem by creating a new department or business to maintain the problem fixes rather than developing a prevention method.

But there are actions for businesses to implement to adapt, evolve, and succeed in the transformation occurring now.

Corporate Social Responsibility (CSR)[5]: More and more companies are increasing how much money, time and effort they are committing to give back to society—and, it is admirable. Changing any part of the business methods and budgeting formula takes a lot of work, and can be disruptive to employees, customers and stakeholders. Many universities are expanding education opportunities in future

---

5   A self-regulating business model that helps a company be socially accountable—to itself, its stakeholders, and the public.

sustainability and humanitarianism, with programs such as ASU's "Responsible Research and Innovation Project," MIT's "Sustainability Initiative" and Stanford's "Social Innovation Review." Many nonprofits are creating Social Impact Indicators in order to quantify, rate and honor those businesses that take leadership roles in committing to the common good, such as "B Lab." And, recently there have been a number of studies showing businesses that score high on "Social Responsibility Indicators" gain higher loyalty from customers within their market. There are also measurable effects on employee job satisfaction and retention which, of course, have a positive effect on the bottom line as well.

Business Environmental Sustainability: We use the term "carbon footprint" generally to encompass all the harmful greenhouse gasses emitted into the atmosphere, as well as the degradation of planetary soil, forests, water, biodiversity, and so on. Form a committee at work to review the ecological impact of the following areas: business methods, office buildings, direct stakeholders, suppliers, local community, vendors, and indirect stakeholders. Research the up-front costs and the long-term savings to reduce your work carbon footprint, then put a plan in place to address each element. Start with implementing the cheap and easy "quick wins." When they incorporate these corporate stewardship measures, virtually every company that has quantified and published their results has experienced one or more of the following: new savings, higher profits, richer customer loyalty, new business opportunities, increased employee retention, and reduced sick days.

Employee happiness, engagement, wellness, development, culture, and perks: Most Americans spend at least a third of their waking hours at work these days. Businesses have at the very least an opportunity—and perhaps a duty—to create for employees an environment that is challenging, fair, and responsive enough to accommodate family, health, and other personal issues when they arise. For ideas, check out www.3talliance.org/perks.

3T Business Social Capital Rating System: Rate business on a scale of zero to three based on its perceived impact in Reputation, Employees, Sustainability, Community, Universality, and Economics. You can rate your business according to the 3T (Think Tomorrow Today) scale in less than two minutes at www.2020theory.org.

Executive Salary Caps: 2020 Theory proposes an annual individual income cap of $6 million to achieve its objectives (inclusive of benefits, commissions, etc.). This is NOT a popular idea. But it only affects anyone *planning* to make more than $6 million PER YEAR, because the 300,000 people or so who currently earn $6 million or more every year are grandfathered into their situation. They are simply encouraged to redefine living standards and reconsider how they spend their grandfathered opulence. This is going to have to be a decision that businesses make for themselves and that someday will be governed by watchdog businesses with no real means of enforcement other than the purchasing shift of the consumer. Any hidden C-Suite[6] side

---

6   A term used to describe corporate officers and directors. The term is derived from the use of the letter C in most high-level positions, such as Chief Operating Officer.

benefits, investments, offshore accounts, and loopholes can be addressed later—this is just a start. Governments may then follow suit one day with regulation, since governments are often reactive instead of proactive.

Business Ethics: In this day and age, technology has fostered a lot of oversight of business practices. Regulatory bodies are getting better at ensuring businesses meet certain standards. Plus, consumers have the power to shut a business down simply by way of online reviews and social media memes. Standard measurements in Social Impact Investing could be expanded to all businesses. Of course, state and federal regulators sometimes introduce fees, more red tape, and more complications that can end up creating inefficiencies worse than the potential harm they are trying to prevent. With the help of A.I. and Open Sourcing in the 2030s, all this can be streamlined.

Business Profits: Companies that earn enormous revenues end up injecting most of those earnings back into the economy. This is a good thing. They hire lots of people, they purchase lots of products and services that support other businesses and people, and they contribute a lot to charity. Still, it is not enough. Unless companies give back more, we as a nation are headed in a bad direction economically and socially. And, of course, businesses should keep some net funds for rainy days and sustainability. That is easily doable with a plan that calls for businesses in the NEAR future to distribute 20% of their net profits among the people within the organization or the local community. This should be a different line item from philanthropy and employee benefits and perks. Businesses should not increase prices; just shift their spending and mindset. By year 2030, business profits will become a hot topic and will be more transparent to the public. Businesses that cap profits at 5% (before the wave of mass criticism) will be rewarded by the spending habits and networks of conscious consumers.

Business Philanthropy: Businesses need to commit at least 1% of total revenue directly to charity in order for conscious consumers to buy from them. This could be done by reducing the advertising budget correspondingly. This seems small and common sense to the average person, but is a HUGE deviation from typical business methods in the current economy. Most Fortune 500 companies donate around half a percent or less of their total revenue to charity, which ends up being millions of dollars, but they often spend between 2% and 20% on advertising which ends up being billions of dollars. The annual revenue of all American businesses combined totals $35 trillion. If those businesses were to commit to set aside JUST 1% of that revenue to charitable causes, the total would equal $350 billion, an increase of nearly $300 billion. This is a no-brainer. Businesses can make a huge impact by merely doubling their charitable giving, and hardly flinch if they reduce their ad spend to cover the cost of doing so.

Note: Philanthropies are not the solution to all problems in the world, but strengthening them immediately will help to improve community resources and weather the impending wave of income and job disruption. Philanthropies, too, need a major system overhaul, but we can focus on that after year 2030.

Business Budgets: Business leaders may have greater responsibility than they realize to affect societal and environmental outcomes. Should leaders fail to step up, then consumers and government may need to force businesses to change their ways to an even larger focus on Social Capital. Otherwise, the profits of antiquated business models may sit in banks, derivatives, and ultimately more perks for the top 1% of the top 1%.

I believe the majority of folks at the top of the top are good people with good intentions. Most are business owners and investors, and they often conspire to help save humanity—not to destroy it. But use your empath power for a minute: you give away millions and maybe billions of dollars to charity as is. You worked hard to enjoy the lifestyle you're accustomed to, and now with the help of technology your business and its primary success indicator are exploding with exciting profitability. It's difficult to say "NO!" to more money. These individuals are hooked (just like everyone else) to earning a bigger and better life. Unless change is forced by consumer spending or government regulations, businesses will continue to layoff humans, maximize profits, and donate a modest percentage to philanthropy. And that does not take into account the psychological warfare these companies will engage in using all the really cool new marketing tools on the horizon, such as augmented reality platforms and subliminal ads in every app, entertainment or social medium you see.

Business junk mail: Can you picture a world with zero junk mail and zero spam or fraudulent emails? This is an easy start we should all agree upon. No more bulk mail, EDDM

(Every Door Direct Mail), or unaddressed mail; all newspapers, coupon books, credit card offers, direct mailers, phonebooks and the like must first receive an opt-in request before delivery. Mailers may send an opt-in mailer one time per year per household they select, but they must clearly show an opt-out option.

Stuff: We've reached a point in our history at which surplus outweighs demand. There is too much. Too many options, too many products, too many services, too many advertisements, too much stuff...the list goes on. The choices are debilitating. Humans will continue to progress and make more options and more goods, services, and entertainment. Most of the choices we have today and the choices of tomorrow won't be instruments of our basic survival, but they can add value and self-actualization to our lives. That is, if we have the mental bandwidth to make a choice.

Business Marketing & Advertising: Reducing advertising spending and proportionally increasing charitable giving and employee culture could possibly strengthen companies, motivate employees and enlighten the world. Just as in the cases of Patagonia, Cliff Bar and other companies that held steadfast to their values despite traditional business methodology, someone had to step up and stand out. More CEOs are going to need to be brave and show the world that their companies can grow business even if they reduce their advertising spend and increase their employee and community spend. Companies that forgo telling the world by way of traditional print advertising have countless ways to do so online. They can make YouTube videos, optimize their web presence, generate valuable content and research to truly make the world a better place. If they are making the world better, then employees, customers and the philanthropies they support can help to spread the message digitally and organically.

A couple of questions to ponder:

Can we find what we need, want, and like without traditional advertising?

What would your life be like without advertising?

I dream of billions of dollars moved out of advertising and shifted toward elevating people and communities in need. I hope you, too, can see the opportunity of redirecting significant amounts of money to health, housing and education. Let's begin with condemning and then abolishing any physical advertising such as solicitations and print ads. Eventually you will be able to choose if you want to view digital advertisements, if you want your personal A.I. to suggest products and services, or if you want to block ads altogether. Even digital ads will have less importance in a world not driven by profit; a world when everyone has their basic needs guaranteed and the opportunity to earn additional resources to pay for the products and services they truly want and need.

We can achieve "evolved business models" and "smart governments" by demanding social capital measurements in all the systems that react to us citizens and us consumers. Let's take the Alpha Bet. This is your call to action: Start a new adventure, just choose a starting point and begin taking control.

TRANSFORM CITIZENSHIP

Instead of fighting against the system, let us show the
way. We shall wake up the "powers that be" to open their
minds and their hearts in profound new realizations.
The way forward for humanity requires a balance
of human feelings and scientific logic.

CHAPTER XI

CHOOSE YOUR OWN ADVENTURE

"IT IS NOW TIME FOR YOU TO WRITE A NEW (ALPHA) STORY FOR YOURSELF."

VISION FLIP

Out with the old FIXED MINDSET.
In with the new GROWTH MINDSET.

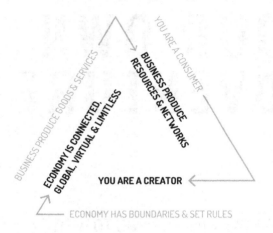

The 2020s decade is a major pivotal moment in human existence. Do you agree? We can force businesses and governments to make things right, but a lot of individuals like us need to start making more changes in their own lives to make it all happen.

We have come to a fork in the road. Machines are now learning what we are doing to the planet. Fortune 500 companies are training many of the Alpha machines to maintain Profitability as their North Star. Meanwhile, global conflicts and environmental issues are driving people out of their homes to find stable shelter, satisfy basic needs and identify any opportunity they might qualify for.

And there's more. During this decade we have the chance to ward off a potential environmental "overshoot and collapse." Millions of people are working on solutions... many of which are not viable without more participation. The Alpha Bet proposes humans can solve nearly all obvious local and global problems within the next 10 years, if the majority of us who realize our power begin to **ACT** in a way that aligns with our true inner values, and if we **TELL** businesses and governments what we want fixed.

A.I. has risen and its platforms (like social media) have "woke" us to many problems. We can view the problems and the many solutions through a new lens. I'm convinced every solution (1) has an expiration date and (2) creates new problems eventually. But that doesn't mean we should stop solving. We can use the tools of today to be a bit more thoughtful about our solutions, to consider the expirations and foresee potential consequences. Doing nothing will just allow the current problems to continue growing.

We know the consequences of sticking to business as usual. We know of the power we hold individually and the emerging technologies at our disposal. It is now time for you to write a new (alpha) story for yourself. One that gradually captures the moment of progress this decade and catapults you into the life of your dreams moving forward. Shall we?

THE ALPHA CHALLENGE

First, take time to stop and think about what you are doing daily and what you would like to be doing. Face your fears, create new traditions, and challenge conventional wisdom. Trust your gut and don't accept "social proof" as a guide. If you have a feeling that something is not right, then pause and listen to that voice. That gut feeling is an invitation to be innovative, to break free from the mold and to create a better way of working, playing, participating and living.

The following challenges will help you do that and help you become an extraordinary Alpha Influencer. The nine challenges fall into one of three categories: **Demand, Declutter, Demonstrate**.

DEMAND

Speak up to government, community and business leaders. Take it as far as you like and start small with "*slacktivism*" (such as signing an online petition), "*craftivism*" (literally creating a craft and displaying it or mailing it somewhere that leaders can see your point of view), or "*RAKtivism*" (see www.RandomActsofKindness.org). Regardless, try to start thinking like a Pro-Activist. As soon as you recognize a problem, kindly and courageously share your thoughts with the powers that seem to be. By the way, this is not a call to complain. It is a call to give constructive feedback in as nice a way as possible.

The wisdom of crowds delivers new and innovative ideas that one leader cannot come up with on her/his own or with a small team. Even A.I. will not achieve human-level **wisdom** for years to come. Good leaders listen to customer and constituent feedback and take action. Artificial Intelligence will help analyze the feedback and organize implementation on a practical and tangible level. But we have to speak up to let our leaders know where we stand, what we expect from them and what we need. How should we do it?

1. Shift consumer demand

Buy from businesses that are truly socially responsible and focus on practices that are environmentally sustainable. Consider what would happen if just 20 million people were to shift their spending habits to influence more companies to be socially conscious. Every dollar counts, and more importantly, the shift in business methodology is the path moving forward. The catch is, you have to switch from a business that is not socially responsible to a different one that is and that you do not already use. In other words, vote with your dollars, your clicks, and your feet; and let other customers know what that can mean.

Imagine if 20 million human Alpha Influencers like you shift a minimum of $20 every month in the same industry. That is $400 million per month per industry. That's enough to make our voices heard. To get maximum impact, shifts need to be grouped by industry. A few places to look online for industry leaders in sustainability is the "SAM Corporate Sustainability Assessment," the "MSCI KLD 400 Social Index," the "Ethisphere World's Most Ethical Companies list," and the "B Corp Directory." Join us and switch some of the suppliers of your expenses each month. Here's the yearly agenda:

- January = Transportation expenses
- February = Television
- March = Food, groceries, restaurants
- April = Insurance
- May = Local businesses such as landscaping, childcare, pest control, home improvement
- June = Personal care, healthcare
- July = Print media
- August = Utilities, housing, investments, Banking, Credit cards
- September = Electronics, computers, cellphones
- October = Entertainment, movies, sports
- November = Apps and online purchases, software
- December = Gifts, apparel, furniture

2. Speak Up Online

If you believe the 2020s decade can be a defining moment in human history, then help to spread the word online. Post any component of The Alpha Bet, such as the Alpha Agreement, 2020 Theory or just your opinion on any topic. Your own blog or website is one possibility, but commenting on a site you don't own is another. One caveat to speaking up online is to be very careful what information you borrow and disseminate...for example, have restraint in sharing something that you haven't verified or your gut feeling tells you it may be false information.

Other ways to speak truth to power include:

- Give constructive feedback via email, social media, and ranking comments.
- Do the research necessary to vote responsibly, not just for candidates but for issues that matter.
- Call out injustice, malfeasance, prejudice and dishonesty.
- Publicly praise those who perform their duties responsibly and even more those who go beyond what is expected.
- Take a step further and speak up offline to help a campaign with "phone banking" via making phone calls to potential supporters. Or "comment banking" via online commenting on articles related to the topic.

3. Propose an Impact Committee at work

All businesses can benefit from having at least one person (or preferably a committee) dedicated to measuring the company's social and environmental impact. Numerous studies have found companies that implement a "triple bottom line" realize greater savings, happier workforce, new revenue generators, and greater profit margins. All of these advances make the idea an honest and easy sell to management.

DECLUTTER

Our purchasing power is a great way to effectively express our wants, needs and expectations. Do you own anything that brought temporary happiness, then sat on a shelf or totally unused for most of the year?

The "Tragedy of the Commons" is that Anthropocene humans are opportunists and will take more than they need. This tilts the equality scale unfairly and ultimately drains natural resources faster than they can be regenerated. A little excess is okay from time to time! Treat yourself to nice things, just be aware of WHY you feel compelled to buy that thing and try to be selective about the company you buy from. We all must be cognizant of the difference between our NEEDS and our WANTS.

It's time we all act fairly as if we're being judged, even when we think we're not being watched. If you are not acting fairly because of your personal morality, spirituality or karma, then do it because you really ARE being watched by businesses and A.I.s everywhere.

4. Reduce, Recycle, Reuse x2

RRR twice as often as you do now...and if possible "Regenerate" (with plants or solar for example). More and more scientists argue that humans are at a pace to over-shoot Earth's resources within 10 to 30 years, which could result in a devastating population collapse that would be felt for decades or even centuries. Specifically, there are some very easy ways to reduce transportation, water, electricity, paper, and plastic usage (such as single-use items, or "fast trash")...plus ways to rethink how to shop, eat, invest and even surf the web.

5. Advertising Feedback

Let at least one business know—by feedback and by your buying habits—how you feel about the barrage of advertisements cluttering your daily environment. At the same time, recognize that **online** advertising may be a necessary component to a healthy societal transformation at this point, since many individuals can make a side income via online advertisers. However, even gig workers who rely on marketing income should soon reconsider their career goals.

6. Buy Less Stuff

It's a consumerism hedonic treadmill we are on together, and it's time our hard-earned dollars aren't wasted. Try to cut your expenses by at least 2% per year. Take control of gift-giving as both the giver and receiver, by concentrating on needs not wants and incorporating gifts to charities instead.

Think before you spend; and, select services that create experiences that continue over time, rather than products that might quickly become obsolete.

DEMONSTRATE

Mass altruism may be the mark of a truly evolved civilization. We'll either reach it this time around, or open the door to a very real possibility of a less-than-comfortable global reset. Humans who worked together were the ones who survived the Ice Age. The next stage in humanity is to work together not merely for survival, but to protect, support and advance the welfare of others. Living according to a creed of virtue takes practice, and even courage, but it does increase happiness and eliminates a lot of problems.

Actively seek out opportunities to help others. Help people you know, and even be open to those whom you do not know yet. Mentor others so they may realize their potential;

or assist someone with the dirty work at the bottom rung, so that they can be closer to fulfilling their dreams.

Volunteering should be another norm, because it is good in two senses: it boosts your personal happiness while you are doing it and helps others in the process. The transition to a society augmented by machines is very likely to produce cultural changes that make community connections more crucial than ever. Philanthropy re-inserts human values and creates a caring exchange. You'll find greater purpose by offering your skills and knowledge, and as any seasoned volunteer will tell you, you usually end up receiving more than you give. And, if you happen to also be teaching, you will—you guessed it—learn more than you teach.

7. Overwhelm Leaders

Email the template letters mentioned in the following section, "Tools To Help," to at least one business and one government leader. This letter is a warning to leaders that you will shift your consumer spending and your support away from anything or anyone harming humanity or planetary resources without reparations. This includes capping future executive salaries at 100 times the average national household income.

For the super wealthy, $10 million USD annual salary (or more) is too much. Presumably, almost everyone agrees with this except those earning $10 million or more annually. Surprisingly, or not, a recent study found 40% of respondents believe there should never be any limit to wealth. Nevertheless, $6 million yearly (relevant to year 2020) is a limit that would allow for greater health, housing and education resources for other employees, citizens (customers among them) and communities when redistributed out of business profits.

8. Share and Volunteer x2

Volunteer twice as often as you do now or at least eight hours per month. Share your time, talents and possessions with anyone you believe is living in a time of need. Consider how you can enable them for success, rather than enable them to remain in a state of heightened needs. Technology can provide for many of our needs as we move into the future, but it will require fewer human workers. If those workers have not been retrained to qualify for other jobs, they are likely to face significant financial restrictions.

The average American who volunteers, spends about 50 hours per year on philanthropy. Let's plan to push the bar and set a goal of four hours per week for 40 weeks out of the year, every year. Making time to volunteer more with nonprofits (even virtual volunteering) will help for-profit businesses configure work schedules to accommodate four-day work weeks as a new societal norm.

9. Demonstrate Health

Change two unhealthy meals per week to a healthier option. And set a goal to exercise _at least_ one hour per week for the rest of your life! This may sound daunting, but it can be reality. Many people do this and if it becomes a permanent lifestyle habit (like brushing your teeth), then you have a better chance at long-term health and happiness, as well as demonstrating a proven way to reduce the nation's healthcare costs.

- A healthier citizenry decreases the government health expenditures, increases economic productivity, and even creates a reduction in crime.
- Some small individual choices can reap large returns. For example, cows are a major contributor to several environmental problems. If you're a burger-binger, try limiting that behavior to evenings only, with the additional goal of eating beef products just once or twice a week next year.
- Take time each day to identify one thing for which you are grateful. Current studies show it will materially improve your mental, emotional and even physical well-being.

TOOLS TO HELP DEMAND, DECLUTTER & DEMONSTRATE

If you want some help deploying some simple actions, I've collaborated with some good people to develop 2020 Theory and the following four resources at www.2020theory.org.

LETTER TO LEADERS: a letter template directed to business leaders for you to send directly. You can copy to use as is, or customize as you like.

2020 THEORY CARDS: a deck of actions and thought experiments to initiate changes in your life and as conversation starters within your networks (i.e. family, friends and acquaintances).

CONSUMERISM RECOVERY PLAN: a methodology for adopting more responsible consumption patterns.

TWO-MINUTES FOR 2020 NEWSLETTER: a weekly newsletter with simple and quick actions each of us can take to make our world a better place. We also love feedback with any suggestions for more two-minute actions that we can share with the subscribers.

Each of the challenges above can open the door to a bigger and better adventure ahead for those who play along. If the challenges and resulting "adventure" do not feel achievable and real to you, then start small by experimenting with some new habits. A simple way to get started in a healthy routine is the Alpha Habits.

Like you, I've got bills to pay and deadlines to meet. But I was stressed out and had my priorities all wrong. I tried numerous incentive systems, self-help books, and accountability apps over the years. Nothing really worked. I went so far as to tattoo symbolic reminders on my body, as well as wearing things meant to ensure I didn't forget to stick to my wellness plan. The problem I found is it's difficult to attempt massive transformation overnight. It is much easier to phase in one thing at a time in order to develop better lasting habits.

ALPHA HABITS

An alpha habit is a NEW habit that makes your life and the world better in some way; and is designed to become permanent.

It's stressful and difficult to make changes when people depend on you...whether it's work-people, family-people, community-people or any other. You're not doing them any good if you are stressed all the time. They are your networks, and you can turn to them when you need a lift. But first you have to fix yourself a little.

Businesses, your property, your bills, your stuff, and your bank do not own you. Your place of work does not own you. Your phone and social media profiles do not own you...Right? Then why do these things control **our behaviors**? We need a cultural shift toward prioritizing our health above all else.

The biggest hurdle may just be giving yourself **permission** to take time for yourself. Like many people, I had been preprogrammed to feel guilty and ashamed of myself when I was not keeping busy and being productive. For me to feel comfortable prioritizing health over finances, I needed to communicate this to my colleagues and my wife. Turns out it was no big deal and they have been very supportive. It took me about three months to start feeling guilt-free for spending three hours a week dedicated to improving myself. But I stuck with it because I began to notice improvements in my mood, memory and wellbeing before the first month was up.

By the way, you'll probably find much of this seems like common sense. Uh huh, then why aren't we all doing this? The key for me was to phase in something new every month. Start simple and get a routine down before moving onto the next month's objective. If you try this, you will know when a new habit is forming, because you feel like something is missing if you skip a habit. If you don't feel that way, then redo the entire month. It's worth it to get this right.

MONTH ONE = MIND

Knowledge. 20 minutes at least two times per week (check out "Blinkist" app or TED talks). After a while begin to seek information you are not necessarily interested in. In addition to widening your knowledge peripheral, this will ensure your technologies don't box you, your habits and behaviors into a category so easily.

Meditate. 10 minutes twice per week. Meditation has been around for millennia, because it works. (I've tried a variety of mantras such as reflecting on love, or energies passing through you, or thinking of absolutely nothing. But my favorite is a Buddhist principle: slowly breath in and think "I am here..." then slowly breath out and think "...for others.") No matter how you meditate, you'll find over time that each method or mantra can affect you in different ways and in different parts of your everyday life.

Hug it out. Hugs and even high-fives send healthy natural dopamine to the brain for a shot of added alertness, happiness, and energy. Hugging has the added benefit of releasing oxytocin in your brain to reduce stress and blood pressure; and studies have found you get the greatest health benefits with eight hugs per day. If you're not ready for a "Hug Time" every hour like the "Trolls," similar health benefits have been found with just one 20-second hug per day. One BIG caveat to this one: if you become a hugger, be 100% certain the receiver is cool with your affection.

MONTH TWO = SPIRIT

Sunlight. 20 minutes (at least!) outside daily (I started doing this while eating lunch). Take it a step further and commit to spend more time in nature. The Japanese practice "shinrin-yoku," or "forest bathing" by simply walking or sitting in a place surrounded by nature because it is proven to lower heart rate and blood pressure, reduce stress hormone production, boosts the immune system, and improves overall feelings of wellbeing.

Gratitude. Every night say, pray, or write 10 things you are thankful for. Keep it up, and you'll start to get creative and realize there's a lot we overlook that we should recognize and be thankful for.

Affirmation. Raise the Roof every morning! Simply throw your hands up like you just won a million bucks and say "Yes" 10 times every day. Do this! I know it sounds woo-woo, but this is highly effective in lifting your mood and getting the day started right. Many motivational speakers use this technique before stepping on stage. Don't keep it a secret or else it seems stranger than it is. Try getting everyone in your household to do it.

MONTH THREE = NETWORK AND PHILANTHROPY

Face time. Join a networking group that meets in person. Searching www.eventbrite.com is a good start (I joined Net Impact, and we host events primarily designed to help businesses leverage their resources for social good). My place of work, for example, now has Corporate Social Responsibility measures and also commits at least 1% of revenue to charity—all of which selfishly improves my mindfulness levels.

Volunteer. There are more than one million nonprofit organizations in need of volunteers, and that's for a wide range of tasks and purposes. Americans who volunteer average about 50 hours per year. How difficult would it be for you to be above average? Can you aim to double that average with two hours per week? Would your place of work support you in that endeavor? If you can't volunteer in person search online for "online virtual volunteering."

MONTH FOUR = BODY

Exercise. At least 20 minutes, two times per week to start. No need to sign up for a program; you just need to get started. You will naturally begin to challenge yourself and push your progress after a while. If you miss a day, no problem, just don't miss any the next week. (For me, mornings don't work and evenings I help put the kids to bed—so I use the middle of the day. I take an hour and half lunch break in the middle of the day to exercise, shower, eat and then get back to work).

Healthy Food. More fruits and veggies seem to be the key. Don't get sleepy or "hangry" during the day. Eat a light lunch and try out "Meatless Mondays." (I keep almonds and healthy snacks near me, eat salad or soup lunches usually, and often only have meat during dinner.)

Water. They say drink half your weight in ounces each day (i.e. five pints a day for a 160 lb. person). Get with the reusable water bottle movement and take one with you wherever you go. (Plus, I have three timers on my phone each day that remind me to drink 16 oz of water and take vitamins. I have found dehydration led to headaches, and moodiness.)

Sleep. Study after study says seven or eight hours of sleep is the perfect amount for a healthy mind. If you stay up late, then sleep in late. Don't feel ashamed to get proper sleep.

MONTH FIVE = PRESENCE & ADDICTION

Attention. I had what Buddhists call a "monkey mind": I was constantly swinging mentally between multiple subjects. One solution is to notice you are doing that and will the subject to leave your mind the way you might watch a cloud go by. And whether monkey mind or your phone is the culprit, when anyone is speaking to you, direct all your attention there.

Family. Make time for family. In the big scheme of things, they may be what's most important to you whether you realize it or not. Go the extra mile and expand your definition of "family" to include someone who has no family.

Neurotransmitters. Dopamine, oxytocin, serotonin and endorphins...most animals will go great lengths to activate feel-good chemicals like these in their bodies. We humans are capable of resorting to methods that often lead to addiction. Drugs, alcohol, and smoking can lead to obvious suffering, but perhaps more common, yet less diagnosed, are behavioral addictions like working, shopping, and video games. How about your phone and social media? How much time do you spend on these technologies in an average day? Are they improving your life at the current rate? Social media, for example, should augment social interaction and not replace it. Consider trying out an Internet-free week-end, or even full on dopamine fasting[1].

What could be nudging your life out of balance? Get a partner to help you quit, set the rules, and keep the poten-tial addiction out of reach. I was constantly checking my various work emails. So my wife and I now keep our phones on the charger after 5:30 PM as a rule of thumb.

MONTH SIX = FINANCES

Time. Determine the value of your time. Search online to find any number of quizzes that help with this.

Reduce and Reuse. Save money by simply reducing how much stuff you buy and how much stuff you throw out (such as food waste). Especially consider cutting back on things that end up sitting in a closet or garage for 11 months of the year. Also, be sure you aren't paying any subscription services (like apps) that are going unused. Finally, another easy way to save a little and do some good is to reduce your energy bills. Search online for "UN SDG Lazy" to learn some easy ways to save on utility bills.

---

1   (a.k.a. stimulus control) A mindfulness practice to abstain from anything that brings pleasure in order to better appreciate and acknowledge dopamine triggers. Typically involves making a concerted effort, in a set amount of time, to avoid social media and TV.

Share. Join the sharing economy and rent something out...for example, your car when you're not using it (www.turo.com) or your home when you're out of town (www.vrbo.com). What else can you rent out?

Freelance. What talents do you have? There are countless "gig" economy websites now. If you can do something remotely or on video, your audience could be any one of billions of people online in the world. Anyone can make money creating Voice Command Skills for devices like Alexa. People are even making money these days selling virtual items in games like Second Life.

Work upgrade. Improve your place of work with Corporate Social Responsibility (CSR) metrics and suggest you get paid more to manage and measure your improvements. An impressive software called "Wespire" is worth exploring. And you can find even more ideas on the Business Assessment at www.2020theory.org.

Invest. If you have money left over, invest it responsibly, such as with a conservative CDFI bank investment like "C-Note." Or, invest in something with higher risk, but potentially better returns such as crowdlending like "Seed Invest" or "Fundrise." A middle-ground investment may be crowdfunding, but typically your investment results in receiving a product or benefit other than a cash. The rule of thumb (and take it or leave it) is to place the largest quantity in the safest investment, a little less in the middle ground, and the least amount into the riskiest venture.

READY, SET, GO!

All this is just a starting point. It began to open doors for me and introduced me to better habits. I now spend a lot more time outside, get more exercise, meditate more, focus more time on my family and not so much time stressing in general.

There is yet to be a magic pill that will give you wellness. Just get started. Twenty minutes per week toward your goal is a success. Sticking to it for more than a month is a huge victory toward a new happy, healthy lifestyle instinct. Then, once you get the routine down, you can start to experiment with the latest mind, body, spirit craze if you want.

Your goal may be to quit an addiction, get more sleep at night or to simply drink more water. Whatever it is, do it! You are not going to be at your best performance for yourself, family and the world if you are operating on a low battery. Start a lifestyle of maintaining a healthy mind and body first, then you can be more productive and better suited for financial improvement.

Accept the fact that this is something you will do. Commit to a starting point right now (like 20 minutes of meditation per week) because in a about five seconds you're going to come up with an excuse not to....

5...4...3...2...1.

We all do that. You only need to START with 20 minutes per week for many of the activities and then try to extend that time each month. Eventually, you may only need to make room for three or four hours per week in total...that may seem like a loss of productivity, but counterintuitively, it will make you stronger, more productive, and at the same time open up the doors of opportunity. As an added benefit, all this is preventative and you will likely save even more time (and money) **in the long term**.

You have less than seven days to begin. So get your phone and set the alerts right now (or if you're reading this closer to year 2030, then voice command this to your door, glasses, T-shirt button or whatever device keeps your calendar). Add Month One habits to the next four weeks on your calendar.

Next, tell someone you are on a mission to create new habits and ask that person to hold you accountable. For added motivation, try this: give that person six $20 bills. Tell them if you succeed each month, then they keep $20 each month. If you feel like your habits for the month aren't sticking, then be honest and tell your chosen person to leave the $20 somewhere where a complete stranger will find it. We are more likely to stick to a goal if someone we care about gets rewarded, rather than ourselves. And it's even more powerful if there is a punishment to the person you care about in case you do not succeed, such as they match your monetary motivation. The reward/punishment doesn't have to be money either. You can get creative and maybe your person will join you, too.

Having a partner in transformation will give you added encouragement to follow through. And the more actions you take, whether it be Alpha Habits or any of the nine

Alpha Challenges, the greater the impact on your life story this decade as we progress through many local and global transformations together. As a byproduct, others will follow and businesses, the government and the Alpha Gen will have to adapt to the lifestyle choices we exhibit, as well.

CHAPTER XII

THE
BEGINNING

"NOW IS NOT THE END. IT IS NOT EVEN
THE BEGINNING OF THE END. BUT IT IS,
PERHAPS, THE END OF THE BEGINNING."

- WINSTON CHURCHILL

YOU MADE IT! You know how to defeat complacency, how to change business as usual, and how to identify marketing tactics designed to steal your attention. But there is one more incredibly formidable beast in your way...the Haters. Haters are people who are inconsiderate, instinctively negative and openly critical of any change to status quo without first investigating the facts.

A particularly troublesome breed of Hater is the "troglodyte" (a term coined by musician, Corey Taylor). I try not to be too much like Captain Planet or too judgmental in general, but I witnessed a guy the other day literally walk out of a store, take his stuff out of the bag, throw the receipt and the bag on the ground, and drive off. This guy is a troglodyte, a person who purposely or obliviously makes things worse for everyone else.

So many ridiculous rules, fine print, regulations and laws are the direct result of governments and businesses trying to protect the general population from these one-off incidences wherein troglodytes screw things up for everyone else.

Furthermore, these Haters are people who are stuck in the old ways. The people who will not change until it's too late. The people who take advantage of your kindness. And, the people who are just having a bad day and project it onto you. Let's add to the list some grownup problems both Alpha Generations don't deal with yet...institutions that charge you big monthly bills (utilities, rent, mortgage, lease, etc) and the people who require you to get a time-intense job done in a short amount of time (deadline droppers).

First, try not to be one of these people. The fact is, we still live in a world where the majority operates by the old rules, and so we must adapt from time to time. It's far easier to avoid becoming a Hater, than it is to avoid them in your life.

- Remember to listen more; and act in a way that demonstrates a new and better way of living.
- Send Haters to www.2020theory.org and spread the word.
- Surround yourself with more mindful Alpha Influencers.
- And, if all else fails, find a way to stay as far from the Haters as possible.

You cannot tell people The Alpha Bet and expect they'll understand it. You have to show them your Alpha Bet choices.

Here's an even tougher opposition to what you want in life...YOU. Are you actually a Hater? Do you believe society and the planet is doomed; or do you understand the massive changes that are necessary (and are beginning) to take place in the world today? Are you critical of yourself when you dream of big change in your life? Are you holding yourself back from the change you want? No doubt you've made mistakes along your life journey. We are human. Give yourself permission, or if necessary go get permission, to move on and focus on today. Then get to work mapping your future goals.

Do you see what you want out of life, but consistently fall back into routine instead of doing what it takes to make it happen? You know you need to eat healthier; you know you need to exercise more and maybe get a new job... maybe you think about these things all the time but you haven't ACTED. You're too busy, got to pay the bills, etc.

We are expert excuse-makers. There IS a way to see the big picture. There are lots of ways to take micro-actions that begin to change your subjective reality and also begin to alter the constructs you interact with. Play along with everyone's view of the world, but in the meantime create the world you want. A new world is forming and so you are just getting ahead of the transformation. Making an Alpha Bet is a way to be prepared for the impending rewrite of the way we interact with **social networks** personally and in your communities, **economic systems** in business and at work, and **political frameworks** in government and laws.

These words will not be enough to get you motivated. Mentally you are READY, but physically manifesting these thoughts into action is like swimming upstream to get a drink of water. You can sit back and drink the water everyone is swimming in and you'll be just fine...or you can fight the current to get something fresh. In this metaphor, the current is your "id[1]," your inner monologue that will quickly shift from "This is what I must do!" to "Why bother, because this world works for me as is."

If you take only one piece of advice from this book, check out www.2020theory.org and sign up for the newsletter. Sounds like a lot of shameless plugs for that site, but it's free and I did work hard with a group of people who care deeply about the future of humanity to come up with simple, experiential, and effective ways to drive the transformation we all desire.

---

1   In Freudian theory, the division of the psyche that is totally unconscious and serves as the source of instinctual impulses and demands for immediate satisfaction of primitive needs.

NOW WHAT?

We know the Alpha Gen is a major catalyst for change in the near future. We know that they can create a world of Abundance. We know they are watching and learning from us.

We know there are a lot of ALPHAS to consider. You can apply "alpha" to anything new with the potential to grow into something great. I'm sure you've noticed the word being used once or twice (or exactly 438 times) in this book! Another way to think about all this is to replace the word Alpha with "new." You are a NEW **influencer** for the NEW **generation** of A.I.s. We must nurture NEW **values** and apply them to a NEW **agreement** as a guide for the development of these smart technologies. It's important now more than ever to flip our perception of the way we do things and see with NEW **vision**. If you have ever bet the world is going downhill, then take a NEW **bet** that forming NEW **habits** in your life is all it takes to make the world better. And there are a variety of NEW **challenges** to take agency in the life you will live in the near future.

The point is this is just the beginning of an exponentially better world, and each of us can have a new lease on life.

The Alpha Bet is not applicable to everyone at all times. Sometimes you have to deal with a massive problem right in front of you in any way you can. But if you are in that sweet spot, the time when you have your health, your needs, and your focus; and are in a place that you are capable of peering outside of personal day-to-day matters, even a little bit, then

273

you have an exceptional window of opportunity. Take advantage of it, and set the wheels of change in motion in your life. It all starts with the thoughts in your head. There have been many psychological studies on two frames of mind:

1. Scarcity mindset describes what is at work when you feel like a victim, if you're often tense, overwhelmed and closed-minded.

2. Abundance mindset occurs when you take control of your life, you are calm but alert, engaged and always open minded.

Which are you?

The 2030s can be a Global Renaissance Period. A rebirth. We are simply at the beginning of this new world of greater efficiency, harmony and abundance. Currently, our collective understanding of the world is changing and some people, businesses, and governments are having a hard time with this. The fact is, it's happening. Now is the time to develop a new foundation of understanding built on 2020 Theory principles and Alpha Vision, or the like. The 2020s is a time of learning, networking, and strengthening this foundation.

Practice seeing though the new lens of reality. Are the constructs around you adapting to the true nature of our global, technological, and societal paradigms? Are these constructs really holding you down? Is the door of opportunity open, but you haven't yet stopped to breathe and see it right in front of you?

The Alpha Bet is that we humans will not just survive, but we will thrive. Taking the Alpha Bet requires conscious choices to shift the paradigms and the algorithms that reinforce Consumerism and Profit as top human values to what we really desire: Health, Happiness and Humanity as our top values. It requires a commitment to change at least one thing about your life, permanently. Considering everything you know now, what is the first action you will take for your Alpha Bet?

Taking the Alpha Bet makes you one of the few superheroes (or Jedi Knights, I prefer) of the world. If you choose to be hopeful and positive about the future, then think in terms of that popular "A" word: **Abundance**. Our world can stay Abundant in all things amazing. We're headed on the right path, and we just need to maintain the momentum in this direction. The alternative is another "A" word, but this one rhymes with Metropolis (kinda: it's apocalypse). And, like Clark Kent, you don't need to be Super all the time—just when it counts.

Be prepared for the opportunity to transform the world. Remember to train yourself to view the world differently and reference the 2020 Theory Tenets if you need some inspiration.

Here are three simple superpowers you possess that can cultivate Abundance in your personal health, purpose, and belonging that can produce a wake of positive impact: Share, Buy, Vote.

#1 You have superpower as part of a local network, so **SHARE** more of your time with community philanthropies. Go the extra mile and share your values with your friends, family and coworkers. Ask them to take the 20 Question Business Workshop in the Resource page at www.2020theory.org.

#2 You have superpower as a consumer, so **BUY** from companies that value philanthropy and people over profits. Go the extra mile and research businesses that are environmentally conscious. Join those of us who are strategically moving money away from companies that are harmful to society at www.3talliance.org/2020mission. And if you want, email or mail the Letter Writing Template to business leaders found in the Resource page at www.2020theory.org.

#3 You have superpower as a citizen, so **VOTE** for leaders and politicians who understand The Alpha Bet message. Go the extra mile and email or mail The Alpha Agreement found in the Resource page at www.2020theory.org.

Sure, someone else will do something to keep the world Abundant. You don't need to do anything, right? There are 250 million adults in the U.S. alone, and plenty subscribe to a methodology or philosophy to make the world an even better place.

"I'll wait until there's an easier way. I'm busy."

No! Dammit. This is it. This is the easiest way. The only way all this works is if lots of people like YOU act upon this message and become a conscious Alpha Influencer. Even if you are an avid environmentalist and philanthropist—thank you, first, but also—this is your call to ramp up your efforts even more. We are out there and we are ready to step up with you. All of us who are conscious and capable of driving this change need to increase our efforts during this decade for maximum effect. Success for 2020 Theory is when we reach 20 million believers who also take action and keep on doing it.

GET MAD!

Are businesses and the government investing in America and creating more human jobs that pay a living wage? The math doesn't add up. Too much money is still getting concentrated in places that do nothing to support a happy, healthy society. Technology will become more efficient and less costly than human workers. New gig-jobs and high-skill jobs will arise, but it may be a very difficult transition for those in low-skill jobs. We may fight it as long as we can, but it will be a painful fight with a brutal ending if we don't accept the facts. Pandora's box is open, and technology isn't going away. It's getting better and it's getting smarter, so let's join forces with technological advancements rather than becoming its bitter enemy.

I'm angry. You're angry too. Channel that energy into action. You read this book for a reason. This is your moment. Here's a quick exercise: think of a movie that made you want to do something amazing for the world or to conquer a big obstacle in life...

Once you have that, then think of a song that gives you strength and confidence when you listen to it. Better yet, find that song right now and play it...

Can you capture the feeling you get from that movie and that song and make that feeling a reality in your day-to-day life? Can you truly take action to break out of routine and become a warrior for something bigger than yourself? The opportunity exists right in front of you. Join us and let's see where this goes. Let's see how deep the rabbit hole is.

Remember, the goal is to force change and become an advanced society by way of knowledge and working together to support community, business, and government Social Capital platforms. We need power in numbers. We need to show a shift in societal demands, not exhibit physical might.

When I think about the future, I am hopeful because I know most humans naturally WANT a better world for all. I know of the tools we have, all the innovation taking place, and I know there are millions of people doing a lot of good. But then I see people suffering in the news and homelessness in my community, I see businesses doing anything to make a dollar, and a bombardment of marketing everywhere. I see nations and politicians acting like children, and troglodytes taking advantage of people who are kind.

It is incredibly upsetting to see all the opportunity for extraordinary positive changes on a global scale, but the massive complacency pushing back against it. According to the "Diffusion of Innovation Theory," it will take a divergence of 13.5% of a population to change the whole. There are plenty of innovators in the world working to excite and activate various populations to the idea of a healthier, more peaceful and more inclusive world on the horizon. The 2020 Theory movement will gain the momentum it needs among people age 18 to 44 in the U.S. once it reaches a critical mass of about 20 million early adopters. Elevating humanity with a global phenomenon that sticks will eventually require nearly all the various movements to converge behind one crystal clear vision that reaches one billion early adopters. Currently, the most effective way to reach 20 million people is the combination of an organic word-of-mouth and social media movement along with resorting to advertising this message to kickstart the 2020 Theory and get more people to take an Alpha Bet. It will take a network effect[2] and it really starts with TWO. If you tell two people and they tell two people and it goes on like this, we can reach 20 million people fairly quickly. If this goes on 42 times, then theoretically we can reach half the population of the world. (And for "Hitchhiker's Guide to the Galaxy" fans, we know that 42 is the answer to the ultimate questions of life, the universe and everything.)

It's amazing how just about anything can go viral nowadays. Unfortunately, panic and fear spread faster than peace and kindness, but all are contagious **for certain**. There are so many sources of "Globalization 4.0" information, and so many "change agents" and "impact leaders." In particular, it is truly awe-inspiring to see the drive the millennial generation has to change the world for good. On the whole, they

---

2   The effect described in economics and business when the value of a product or service increases according to the number of others using it.

are doing it, and we all need to get on board to magnify the efforts taking place now.

What does the Alpha Gen think of you? Are you inspiring greed or **generosity**, waste or **moderation**, fear or **courage**, indifference or **empathy**, division or **collaboration**, uniformity or **diversity**, hatred or **humanity**. The Alpha Bet is a launching point and an invitation to join the war on complacency, to edit and build upon the plan as we go—but more than anything to act and to act now before the window of opportunity passes us by.

WIN THE ALPHA BET

We all have greater influence and more capabilities than we know. Humans are pretty damn smart. We just need to tap into our specific talents. How smart are we?

Medically, we can give sight to the blind and hearing to the deaf now. We can look at every part of your chromosomes and DNA to know your exact genetic makeup. We have medicine that prevents disease and quickly heals ailments. Surgery Bots have already been developed and are being used in hospitals. We have robotic prosthetic limbs, artificial hearts, brain implants to stop seizures, and countless other God-like solutions.

Technologically, you can talk on a tiny cellular phone, and another person can hear you (and see you) in real time from the other side of the planet.

Omnisciently, you have essentially all the knowledge of the civilized world in your hand. You can go to Google Maps, zoom in, and tour almost any town anywhere.

Terrifyingly, we theorized and tested splitting an atom in half to create a five-mile radius explosion 60 years ago and today thermonuclear weapons are suspected to have the power to destroy 40,000 miles in one shot.

Wizardly, if I type on a laptop keyboard, each key is turned into 1s and 0s and it instructs a tiny microchip to open and close receptors in a sequence that is converted by a tiny processor to show me certain digital images pieced together on my computer from thousands of tiny pixels. And then, I save the images and log on to my email to send them through the Internet where electromagnetic frequencies send oscillating waves of information at the speed of light to a satellite. That satellite, which is receiving millions of signals, then shoots down my message and images to precisely the laptop on the other side of the planet I have designated, and that computer decodes all the information without a single error.

Rapidly, IBM's Watson computer analyzed more than 70,000 academic articles in 2014, leading to the discovery of six proteins that are being targeted for new cancer research. This discovery would have taken one human scientist 38 years to accomplish if she read five academic papers per day. And in 2020, you can ask a question to Google "Talk To Books," which will then read every word of 200,000 books in less than one second to come up with an answer.

Humans thought all this up, figured it out and made it reality. Humans can solve human problems. The problems we face are just puzzles we need to sit down and figure out.

Our monkey brains get frustrated and just want to blow stuff up. We can't do that right now. We need to have restraint, at least until we get back on a path of survival as a species.

We cannot fear action. <u>We cannot fear change at this moment in history.</u> In many circumstances, especially when an idea, program or invention creates change for a large number of people, we are really good about studying and analyzing and researching and investing more time and money into what the possible outcomes will be. After a few solutions are proposed, then it is time for someone to be brave and "DO."

All individuals whatever their nationality, education, status, race or genetic heritage need to stop...think...and then act. As of right now, many scientific, psychological, sociological, economic and philosophical indicators point to a path of mass destruction at some point in human civilization on Earth. We can only estimate how long it will take. Maybe our Earth and our species will survive for billions more years...or it could only be for 50 more years. I believe we have billions of years to go, and the next 50 could be incredibly prosperous—if only we set ourselves up for success during this time of transformation right now, before 2030.

If everyone just lived, worked, and consumed purely for their own self-interest, then our species would be in trouble. If no one cared, then maybe a few people could make it off of this planet intact. It really is not too much of a stretch to say we can soon start to populate another planet. Some things in this book sound like science fiction. They aren't. This is very real. The problems are real, and Stage One of the solution begins for you today. Humanity and planet Earth have a lot of obvious issues, but even more opportunities for you to become part of the solutions.

Maybe someone will someday have an extraordinary idea for a government policy, or a business method, or a community program that can reverse extreme inequality and environmental catastrophes. Maybe that person will be too late. Maybe you have the idea and the opportunity to help force change before we pass the point of no return?

The largest piece of the puzzle is how to get everyone to agree. Everyone agrees to use the Internet because it adds value to our lives and helps us function according to the constructs of society today. It didn't happen overnight, though. Now we need to follow the plan to alter the constructs so that everyone gradually joins in and agrees to use Social Capital.

Humanity now has all the resources we need to end poverty, suffering, disease, and debt. We have the technology to eliminate fine print, waste, decision fatigue, and planned obsolescence. Accepting profit motives, high interest rates, advertising, and deadlines in our lives is holding us back from true progress. The ways of the 20th century were reactive fixes, fear, control, "modern" warfare, and the Anthropocene. We can evolve as a species this century if our actions reflect our values and if we ensure technology is truly honoring and supporting those values.

Will we win The Alpha Bet? You will see many transformations happening this decade. YES, humans will use their newfound powers to change the world for the better. I believe humanity will become healthier and happier because enough of us humans are eager for drudgery, inequalities, and ecological problems to end and willing to take action to begin a revolution in global health, happiness, and opportunity. But the work has to be done this decade while exponential technologies are still malleable to be of greatest benefit to humanity, rather than greatest benefit to profit margins.

This is the decade of massive transformation, and we know change is hard. Each of us can embrace change to give new **purpose** to our lives individually. You win The Alpha Bet when you refocus your energy away from "How can I earn more money?" to "How can I use my time and resources to change the world?" You win when your technologies augment your Alpha Vision. And, you win when you see past the cognitive filters that blind us—and operate with 20/20 clarity.

The Alpha Bet is a prediction. Many of our pre-2020 social constructs will change. If enough people alter their behaviors before year 2030, then we'll begin to enjoy new social norms in areas such as these:

PERCEPTION

Emerging technologies will allow you to literally perceive the world in new ways. Your five principal senses can be amplified with wearable technology soon. And many new "senses" can be downloaded to your wearable tech to accurately perceive anything from air quality to detecting various dangers to knowing if a person is being truthful or lying.

Moreover, advances in medical and agricultural biotech will help us to feel healthier and mentally sharper; to sleep better, and to feel less pain without side effects. All of these technologies are coming soon and will rapidly become widely acceptable, affordable and abundant.

Schools will place a greater focus on self-actualization skills such as easily finding individual purpose without the lens of social proofing. The Alpha Gen will augment our ability to identify when our cognitive shortcuts are helping or hurting our subjective view of reality. And, increasingly this decade, you will have greater ability to be present and perceive what is right in front of you more clearly instead of being distracted too much by thoughts about the past or future. You will also get to choose to accept advertisements in your life, or to live ad-free (at the cost of giving up personal data). In the 2030s, data and your time will be given a value worth as much or more than money today.

FINANCES

Society agrees on the value of fiat currency and soon we shall agree on the value of Social Capital. This will be a topic that will gain traction over the coming years and before long, you will be rewarded for being a trustworthy person, for sharing, for volunteering, and for meeting your health goals. How you spend your time to help society (including helping yourself to be a balanced, healthy and happy member of society) will earn you more time and access for enhanced basic needs.

Alpha Gen automation will become ubiquitous in every business and the cost of goods and services will lower;

meanwhile essential services will become more valuable. Opportunities to obtain multiple credentials and certifications within essential services of the near future can broaden your financial and capability horizon. Wealth will eventually be redefined and money can serve a new purpose. In the meantime, a growing cultural shift from material consumption toward spending more on experiences will enhance our general quality of life.

LIFESTYLE

"Quality of life" means different things to different people, but we now have the data to improve lives across demographic and cultural divides. The trends of simplicity and mindfulness will continue to be embedded into our lives and will be a cornerstone philosophy for the Alpha Gen. Experiential learning of life skills and collaboration skills will gain importance in youth education curricula. Experiential entertainment (such as art, music, sports, recreation and gamified exercise) will define you more than the stuff you own or the job you do for money.

Unconscious biases will still be an inherent human trait for a while, but managing biases and retracting income, racial and gender inequality gaps will take center stage—inciting higher levels of equality and respect in a rapid "network effect," soon. Prioritizing individual health and wellness will become a key steppingstone toward healthier communities and environment.

SURROUNDINGS

You, your local community, your digital communities, and also your physical environment all have needs. You will soon have more opportunities to give back to your various surroundings in return for the benefit you receive from them. An increase in volunteerism will improve your surroundings in countless ways...especially when the concept of "placemaking" is a normalized mantra. The Alpha Gen will further help reconceive communities this decade with data to support "Freedom of Attention" and refining "Social Determinants of Health."

Nature's resources need time to regenerate and so managing this will become a new norm. We all need Natural Capital such as clean water, fresh air, healthy food, and sustainable shelter. In a few years from now, you'll be guaranteed a basic allotment of these things in exchange for doing your part in protecting your local ecosystem. Supporting your surroundings is your new chief role in society instead of your job.

WORKPLACE

Your place of work is primarily a means to earn money to pay for your lifestyle, right now. It can also sometimes give a person a sense of greater purpose. And some people argue that work keeps our minds occupied and contributing to the social good. The Alpha Gen will certainly be altering the construct of capitalism so that it genuinely achieves the greatest social good. Work will take on a new meaning, as the "nine to five, Monday to Friday" routine will be a paradigm of the past.

Your place of work will not be "business as usual" by 20th century standards. All businesses will need to be part of the Circular Economy to succeed and will have a defined Social Responsibility function—just as all businesses have an Accounting function. The Alpha Gen will mediate collaboration between formerly competing businesses in order to prudently and proactively improve the world. And many retail stores and malls of the pre-2020s will be converted into community hubs to ensure long-term goals and the needs of nearby communities are being met. What you do to earn money and social capital in the future, can match your values, your "flow state" capabilities, and your potential in order to bring you maximum joy. We will have more time and tools to connect our individual purpose to the greater social good as long as we peacefully participate in the developing rights of citizenship.

CITIZENSHIP

By the end of this decade, you will have a simple way to access very inexpensive and quality education, healthcare, home utilities, transportation, internet, insurance, and basic needs. Governments and communities will use "Systems Thinking" to distribute resources in a way that gives us shared liberty to at least pursue balance in life—as long as we do not tread on the liberty of others. In other words, citizenship will truly free us from worries of limited sustenance or opportunity.

We now know that individual progress is connected to overall human progress. Billions of humans will never agree on one set of ideologies, but the fact remains we all belong to one planet, right now. Alpha Gen technologies will help to consolidate the many metrics of true human progress; and will consider more than just economics such as the Human Development Index and the Social Progress Index. There are very real threats to our lives and livelihood, but as these indices become globally standardized, governments will work together to better protect us individually, and to continue reducing the amount of conflicts and suffering in the world.

The Earth, its inhabitants, and the rules that guide our lives are rapidly transforming. As we humans grow in numbers, as do our differences and our "complexities." But our creativity and our love are also growing in numbers. This is an incredible time like no other in history. This is our moment to rethink everything...and we, the people, have the tools to follow through. Check back here in a few years to determine if the predictions are coming true, if you are adapting to the transforming world, and if we are all on the path to winning **The Alpha Bet!**

The world is complex. It's exciting and beautiful. Simply embrace the complexity and explore your connection to the good in the world.

*If you want a summary of the terminology in this book, visit www.3Talliance.org/vocab

JOIN US

The storm is here but our True North is constant
in a sea of change. Let us be the guiding light illuminating
the way through the darkness of future uncertainty.
We shall protect and guide others with confidence,
compassion and courage.

THANK YOU TO:

3BL Media

Arizona State University, Sustainability Opportunity Cohort

Carbonn Center Climate Registry

Conscious Capitalism

Credit Suisse, Global Wealth Report

Democracy.Earth, "The Social Smart Contract"

EAM, JWM, JAM

Ethical Corp Responsible Business

Global Covenant of Mayors

Global Impact Investing Network, IRIS+

Global Reporting Initiative, "The Transparent Economy"

Good Country Index

International Monetary Fund

International Organization for Standardization

Massachusetts Institute of Technology, Sloan Executive Strategy
    and Innovation

Net Impact

Our World in Data, Human Development Index

Palehorse Design and Artwork

Penworthy, LLC

Poverty Probability Index

Project Drawdown

Singularity University, State of the Global Grand Challenge

Social Progress Index

Social Wealth Economic Indicators

Staci Weber Graphic Design

State of the Future Index

Team Finally: Victoria, Caz, Carly and Franz

The Aspen Institute, FAST SIAMT

United Nations Human Development Report, and U.N. Global Compact

World Economic Forum, The Great Reset

World Future Society, Civilization Development Goals

World Happiness Report

World Health Organization

XEIA.AI

LK ↓ΞVI□ ᄀ،ュᄅ⁻ュᄇ

FUNDAMENTAL CONCEPTS

2020 Theory

A three-stage approach over the course of three decades to ensure humans thrive on a pathway to "Civilization Type One" (CT1 definition). Year 2020 was the beginning. It's the moment when the Earth stood still; and simultaneously when many artificial intelligence software programs surpassed exponential data inflection points while teaching themselves and writing their own algorithms based on programmed boundaries and observable patterns (such as human online behavior and the Internet of Things). Stage One of 2020 Theory is called "The Alpha Bet." It involves transforming patterns and human behaviors to passively train young A.I.s to perpetuate ecological abundance, global peace, and individual human welfare.

Alpha Agreement

A modern refinement of the "Social Contract" theory which describes how a diverse and complex society can function in peace and prosperity. It's an overarching societal agreement that all humans should have certain rights (no matter what), and how these inalienable rights can be maintained and nurtured in harmony with political authority. One requirement is that businesses and governments operate according to the will of the people and not the other way around.

Alpha Bet

A prediction that old social norms, government powers, and business methods are coming to an end and a new set of rules and systems will emerge before year 2030. The reason for this massive transformation is a simultaneous acceleration of global interdependence, environmental solutions, and smart technologies (such as automation and machine learning). The risk is if too many old undesirable concepts are codified into the new way of operating and perpetuate systemic problems. The Alpha Bet is a call to action to mitigate this risk by empowering individuals to apply more of their personal time and resources to contribute to the design of a new and improved world with narrowing inequality gaps and abundant planetary resources.

Alpha Challenges

Beginning to challenge oneself or a friend to change his or her normal routine and take action to change the world. The three "D"s to change the world is DEMAND (such as at retailers, on social media, and at work); DECLUTTER (such as reducing waste, blocking advertisements, and spending less on new products); and DEMONSTRATE (such as contacting leaders as a united front, volunteering more, and making wellness a priority).

DEFINITIONS

Alpha Generation

People born between years 2010 and 2025 who are born into this world of unparalleled technological power, greater global perspectives and heightened socially responsible awareness. (Can also refer to exponential technologies developed during the same period of 2010 to 2025).

Alpha Habits

A new habit that makes your life and the world better in some way; and is designed to become permanent. The Alpha Habit method is to systematically focus on achieving healthy mind, spirit, body, network, presence, and then finances --- in that order.

Alpha Influencer

A person who consciously changes their perceptions, finances, lifestyles, surroundings, workplaces, and citizenship behaviors in a way that diverges from 20th century concepts. The purpose of a human Alpha Influencers is to cause artificial intelligence technologies (such as business marketing, intelligence, and analytics A.I. software) to adapt its algorithms to support true human wellness, peace, progress and prosperity.

Alpha Values

The 12 predominant human values common among many religions, cultures, and philosophies that must also be programmed into artificial intelligence source code whenever possible: self-control, perseverance, forgiveness, happiness, variety, loyalty, courage, truth, love, health, patience, and respect.

Alpha Vision

The practice of perceiving the world and your internal thoughts in a new way. Accepting that the future is not predetermined, there is more good than bad in the world, and there are countless ways to improve almost any situation. Alpha Vision requires an open mind to ideas that oppose your core beliefs, and to consciously self-acknowledge mental shortcuts (such as implicit bias or social proofing). Having Alpha Vision allows one to easily find more alternatives and seek opportunities whenever presented with a limitation or obstacle in life.

GLOSSARY

2ⁿᵈ Order Consequences   **3**
(a.k.a. Second-Order Effects) Are outcomes that are different than the first desired outcome yet are directly related to the initial decision. Every decision has a consequence and each consequence has another consequence.

Agnotology   **135**
The study of culturally induced ignorance or doubt, particularly the publication of inaccurate or misleading scientific data.

AgTech   **196**
Agricultural Technology such as field crop sensors to use exact amounts of water and energy, or to analyze soil health.

Anthropocene   **1**
A period of time (2.6 million years ago to the present), characterized as the time in which the collective activities of homo sapiens began to substantially alter Earth's surface, atmosphere, oceans, and systems of nutrient cycling.

Astroturfing   **207**
The practice of masking the true sponsors of a message or organization to make it appear as though it originates from and is supported by grassroots participants.

Attention Economy   **129**
The theory that the attention span of online users is a limited commodity that is subject to market forces.

Augmented Reality (AR)   **82**
An overlay of computer-generated content on the real world that can superficially interact with the environment in real-time.

Backcasting   **106**
A planning method that starts with defining a desirable future and then works backwards to identify processes that will connect that specified future to the present.

Biohacking   **28**
Biological experimentation (as by gene editing or the use of drugs or implants) done to improve the qualities or capabilities of living organisms especially by individuals working outside a traditional medical research environment.

Biomimicry   **32**
The science of applying nature-inspired designs in human engineering and invention to solve human problems.

Blockchain   **49**

A system in which a record of transactions (such as smart contracts or cryptocurrency) are maintained across several computers that are linked in a peer-to-peer network.

Business Carbon Tax   **231**

A fee that a government imposes on any company that burns fossil fuels. The most widely discussed are coal, oil, gasoline, and natural gas.

C-Suite   **237**

A term used to describe corporate officers and directors. The term is derived from the use of the letter C in most high-level positions, such as Chief Operating Officer.

Citizen Social Capital Points   **48**

A doctrine that the capitalist system does not distribute sufficient income to keep itself in operation; and must issue national dividends, free basic needs services, and/or a monetary equivalent distributed in exchange for participation in activities deemed good for society.

Civilization Type One (CT1)   **72**

A civilization which has mastered and can fully control its planetary energy, information and resources in a way that provides for continued regeneration and distribution systems that support an ever-improving lived experience for all of its inhabitants while managing and mitigating any existential threats. Other theories on Civilization Type One have been proposed by the World Future Society, the Venus Project, Game B, Carl Sagan, and the Kardashev Scale.

Cognitive Bias   **105**

An error in our thinking process that affects our decisions making. As humans, we don't always see things as they really are, or remember things as they really were. As a result, we create our own "subjective reality" that affects our judgment. Exploitation of this human vulnerability is capitalized in various marketing strategies.

Community Representative   **89**

The plan to have trained health and security professionals who live in each community in the U.S. as a resource and as a preventative measure to identify community security or individual health issues proactively. One proposed format is a collaboration between social workers, police, USPS workers, and delivery people. For details, visit www.3talliance.org/reps.

Constructs   **42**

Any theoretical concept, structure or rule that began as an idea and developed into a generally agreed upon system within a group or society at a given time. Examples include social networks, business and economic systems, and political frameworks.

Corporate Social Responsibility (CSR) 235
A self-regulating business model that helps a company be socially accountable—to itself, its stakeholders, and the public.

CRISPR 102
(a.k.a. CRISPR-cas9) Is a gene editing technology that can alter an organism's DNA with a bacteria that can pinpoint and destroy or replace precise DNA sequences. *Notably: The Human Genome Project (HGP), the first whole human genome sequencing in 2000, cost over $3.7 billion and took 13 years of computing power. Today, it costs roughly $1,000 and takes fewer than three days which has allowed CRISPR technology to be affordable.

Data Exhaust 176
(a.k.a. Dark Data) Refers to the trail of data left by the activities of individuals or businesses which is not used to derive insights or for decision making, but the data could hold patterns and predictive solutions (such as computer operations, transactions, online behaviors, geospatial and time data).

Decentralization 207
The spread of power away from one centralized authority or entity such as a bank, a large business or a government.

Decision Fatigue 18
The deteriorating quality of decisions made by an individual when faced with too many choices.

Deepfakes 16
A technique for human image synthesis based on artificial intelligence. It is used to combine and superimpose existing images and videos onto source images or videos with a high potential to deceive.

Dopamine Fasting 263
(a.k.a. stimulus control) A mindfulness practice to abstain from anything that brings pleasure in order to better appreciate and acknowledge dopamine triggers. Typically involves making a concerted effort, in a set amount of time, to avoid social media and TV.

Economies of Scale 217
Reduction in cost per unit resulting from increased production, realized through operational efficiencies.

Emerging Technologies (EmTech) 23
21st century technologies reshaping life as we know it. Examples include: quantum computing, Artificial Intelligence (AI), Extended Reality (XR), Robotic Process Automation (RPA), drones, 3D printing, smart sensors, smart contracts, autonomous vehicles (AV), alternative fuel, biometric ID, synthetic biology, bioprinting, Voice-user Interface (VUI), Brain-computer Interface (BCI), and MUCH more. *Notably includes new tech industries:

PropTech (property), FinTech (financial), EdTech (education), FemTech (female), MadTech (Marketing), InsurTech (insurance), WealthTech, LegalTech, FoodTech, AgeTech...you get the trend.

Experiential Learning **202**

The process of learning through physical experience in a real-world setting using as many of the five senses as possible for greater learning retention.

Extended Reality (XR) **28**

(a.k.a. cross reality) Is an all-encompassing term for technologies that bring digital objects or sensations into the physical world (Real Reality - RR) or vice versa. Examples include Mixed Reality, Virtual Reality, Cinematic Reality and Augmented Reality, Cyborg Intelligence, wearables and sensory interface technologies.

Flock Technology **186**

(a.k.a. swarm intelligence) It is the collective behavior of decentralized, self-organized technology, natural or artificial to work together and share information within a digital "mesh network." Examples include drone coordination and simultaneous localization and mapping (S.L.A.M.) technology for autonomous vehicles.

Fourth Industrial Revolution **155**

A time when technologies blur the lines between the physical, digital, and biological spheres. The First Industrial Revolution used water and steam to power machines; the Second used electricity for mass production; and the Third used information technology for automation.

Freedom of Attention **47**

Coined by Dr. James Williams, co-founder of Time Well Spent campaign, it is the belief that technology should be designed to improve our lives and help its user achieve their goals...NOT to achieve more clicks or engagement with the technology itself.

Global Opportunity Zones **233**

International collaboration to incentivize corporations to invest in specific areas prone to conflict and war via tax and resource assistance. The objective is to improve the land and the livelihood of anyone who would otherwise resort to crime or be recruited into terrorist groups.

Globalization 4.0 **40**

Term coined at the World Economic Forum Davos 2019 summit describing the complete digitization of the social, the political, and the economic—changing the way that individuals relate to one another and to the world at large.

Governing the Commons **46**

When a shared natural resource is governed to allow for collective common good and regeneration rather than self-interest and resource depletion. Coined by Nobel Prize Winner and Economist, Elinor Ostrom.

Great Wealth Transfer   **26**
The period of time between 2020 and 2040 during which 45 million U.S. Baby Boomers are presumed to transfer more than $60 trillion of wealth (collectively) to their children.

Green Certification   **58**
Any number of certifications for social responsibility and particularly environmental sustainability. See examples at www.3talliance.org/certs.

Greenwash   **207**
Disinformation disseminated by an organization so as to present an environmentally responsible public image.

Happy Chemicals   **31**
The four neurotransmitters in our brains most often associated with feelings of happiness: Dopamine, Oxytocin, Serotonin and Endorphins (DOSE).

Hashgraph   **162**
An algorithm to record transactions with a time stamp similar to blockchain but faster. The major difference is blockchain technology is designed to be purely public open source and decentralized while hashgraph is a patented and private algorithm.

Hedonic Treadmill   **128**
(a.k.a. hedonic adaptation) The tendency of humans to make purchase decisions that give temporary dopamine increase, and then the purchase quickly loses its value in personal happiness and becomes an object of clutter.

Id   **272**
In Freudian theory, the division of the psyche that is totally unconscious and serves as the source of instinctual impulses and demands for immediate satisfaction of primitive needs.

Incentive Insensitivity   **32**
Coined by Dr. Vivienne Ming, it is a form of internal motivation to act regardless of external factors like money or reward. It is a necessary component for successful athletes to "get in the Zone."

Least Economically Developed Countries (LEDC)   **194**
Nations that exhibit the lowest indicators of socioeconomic development and low "Human Development Index" ratings.

Most Economically Developed Countries (MEDCs)   **13**
"Most economically developed countries," which are sovereign states that have a developed economy and advanced technological infrastructure.

Moore's Law   **140**
Named after Intel co-founder Gordon Moore, states that processor speeds, or overall processing power for computers will double every two years, meanwhile costs will reduce to the consumer, and this trend would continue for the foreseeable future.

NGO   **162**
   Non-governmental organizations (NGO) are organizations independent
   of any government. They are usually non-profit, and many are active in
   humanitarian or social areas.

Natural Capital   **47**
   The world's stocks of natural assets which include its geology, soil, air, water and
   all living things. It is from this natural capital that humans derive a wide range
   of services, often called ecosystem services, which make human life possible.

Network Effect   **279**
   The effect described in economics and business when the value of a product
   or service increases according to the number of others using it.

Oligopolies   **10**
   A market in which control over the supply of a commodity is in the hands of
   a small number of producers.

Overshoot and Collapse Process   **13**
   (Similar to "Malthusian catastrophe") occurs when a population's demand
   on an ecosystem exceeds the capacity of that ecosystem to regenerate the
   resources. One example is the ecological collapse of the original inhabitants
   on Easter Island.

Pigouvian Taxes   **1**
   A tax on any market activity that generates negative externalities. The tax is
   intended to correct an undesirable or inefficient market outcome.

Placemaking   **230**
   Part of the "maker movement," it is a multi-faceted approach to the planning,
   design and management of public spaces with the intention of promoting
   community health, happiness, and well-being.

Planned Obsolescence   **1**
   A legal practice (in U.S.) and policy of certain businesses that produce
   consumer goods that rapidly become obsolete due to frequent changes in
   design, termination of the supply of spare parts, and the use of nondurable
   materials.

Sustainable Development Goals (SDG)   **6**
   The 17 Sustainable Development Goals (SDGs) developed in 2015 and
   adopted by all United Nations Member States, are a call for action by all
   countries to promote prosperity while protecting the environment.

Sharing Economy   **15**
   An economic model defined as a peer-to-peer (P2P) based activity of
   acquiring, providing, or sharing access to goods and services that is often
   facilitated by a community-based online platform.

Sin-Stinct **184**
Human instincts often identified as one of the "seven deadly sins" known as pride, greed, lust, envy, gluttony, wrath, and sloth. These are also signal emotions that at one point had an evolutionary purpose, but may no longer be useful in the 21st century.

Sixth Mass Extinction **4**
An ongoing extinction event of species during the present Holocene epoch as a result of human activity. The included extinctions span numerous families of plants and animals. *Notably, this extinction is happening at a faster rate than all other mass extinction events before on Earth.

Smart Cities **230**
An urban area that uses different types of electronic Internet of Things (IoT) sensors to collect data and then use insights gained from that data to manage assets, resources and services efficiently.

Smart Contracts **162**
Transactions and agreements facilitated by a digital blockchain ledger and often carried out among disparate, anonymous parties without the need for a central authority, legal system, or external enforcement.

Social Capital **11**
Any activity considered good for society. Often refers to a form of measuring levels of trust, cooperation, sharing, volunteering, and relationship building.

Social Conscription **202**
A government mandated enrollment into authorized philanthropic organizations with limitations as to whom is required to enroll, such as age range and physical ability.

Social Determinants of Health (SDOH) **50**
Identifying and preemptively improving neighborhood environments, economic stability, education, access to medical care, and behaviors toward health on a hyperlocal and individual basis.

Social Engineering **211**
The act of exploiting human weaknesses to gain access to personal information or to psychologically manipulate people into performing actions.

Social Proofing **59**
(a.k.a. behavioral contagion) Is a psychological phenomenon where people assume the actions of others in an attempt to reflect correct behavior for a given situation. Typically an instinctual decision rather than a conscious decision.

Systems Thinking **32**
The opposite of "binary thinking." It involves several iterations of an idea and considers the way that a system's components interrelate, over time, and within a larger system. One example is "human centered design thinking."

Technology Tax   **12**
A fee that a government imposes on any company that replaces a significant number of human workers with technology, such as machine learning software or robotic process automation (RPA).

Tier Three and Tier Four Business   **140**
The theory by George Basile, Senior Sustainability Scientist at ASU, that the next generation of business are founded on sustainable principles. Dr. Basile has identified an evolution of businesses from Tier 1 (such as focused on growth and profit within immediate bounds of business) to Tier 4 (such as using sustainability as an advantage within a global system that can reshape society).

Transhumanism   **72**
The use of sophisticated technologies to enhance human intellect and physiology (such as human augmentation with brain-computer-interfaces, nano-medication, and designer gene therapy).

Triple Bottom Lines (TBL)   **10**
An accounting framework with three parts: social, ecological, and financial. Some organizations have adopted the TBL framework to evaluate their performance in a broader perspective to create greater business sustainability and value.

Virtual Nation (VN)   **12**
Online (or Extended Reality) communities that spend money, time, volunteering, data, or social capital cryptotokens in exchange for citizenry. Citizenship can include an array of benefits such as cybersecurity, education, transportation partnerships, guaranteed highest quality products, food and water security, crime and property insurance, no interest loans, and emergency safe havens like micronations or bunkers.

Virtual Reality (VR)   **28**
A fully immersive computer-generated experience using purely real-world content (360 Video), purely synthetic content (Computer Generated), or a hybrid of both typically viewed through special VR goggles along with wearable technology.

Wisdom of Crowds   **46**
(a.k.a. Crowd Intelligence) Is the idea that large groups of people are collectively smarter than individual experts when it comes to problem-solving, decision making, innovating and predicting.

Zero-point Energy   **71**
The lowest possible energy that a quantum mechanical system may have. Harnessing this energy would mean generating power from the moving molecules, protons, electrons, neutrons, or dark matter within anything (air, object, or being).

YOU ARE NOW AN OFFICIAL HUMAN ALPHA INFLUENCER.
CUT OUT THE FOLLOWING ALPHA BET AMBASSADOR CARDS AND SPREAD THE WORD.

ALPHA INFLUENCER
202-774-2087
www.2020theory.org

Give this card to someone at work.

ALPHA INFLUENCER
202-774-2087
www.2020theory.org

Give this card to a gig-worker or rideshare driver.

ALPHA INFLUENCER
202-774-2087
www.2020theory.org

Give this card to a college or high school student.

ALPHA INFLUENCER
202-774-2087
www.2020theory.org

Give this card to a stranger in a bookstore or coffee shop.

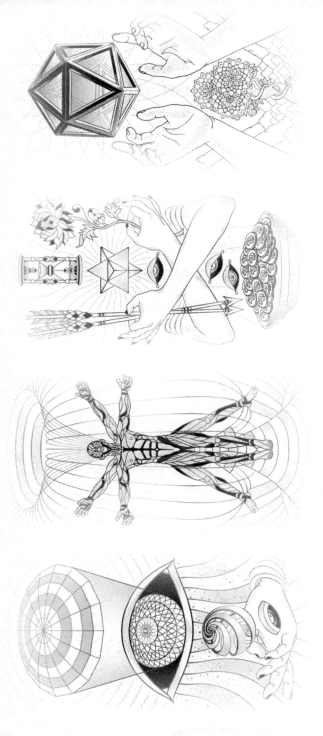

YOU ARE NOW AN OFFICIAL HUMAN ALPHA INFLUENCER.
CUT OUT THE FOLLOWING ALPHA BET AMBASSADOR CARDS AND SPREAD THE WORD.

ALPHA INFLUENCER
202-774-2087
www.2020theory.org

Give this card to a friend.

ALPHA INFLUENCER
202-774-2087
www.2020theory.org

Give this card to any event volunteer.

ALPHA INFLUENCER
202-774-2087
www.2020theory.org

Give this card to a family member.

ALPHA INFLUENCER
202-774-2087
www.2020theory.org

Give this card to anyone you love.

THINK TOMORROW TODAY

Made in the USA
Las Vegas, NV
31 May 2021

23919653R00184